WESTERN MUSIC, MARGARITAS,
OiL WELLS, PINEY-WOODS TALES

KITCHEN
JUNK

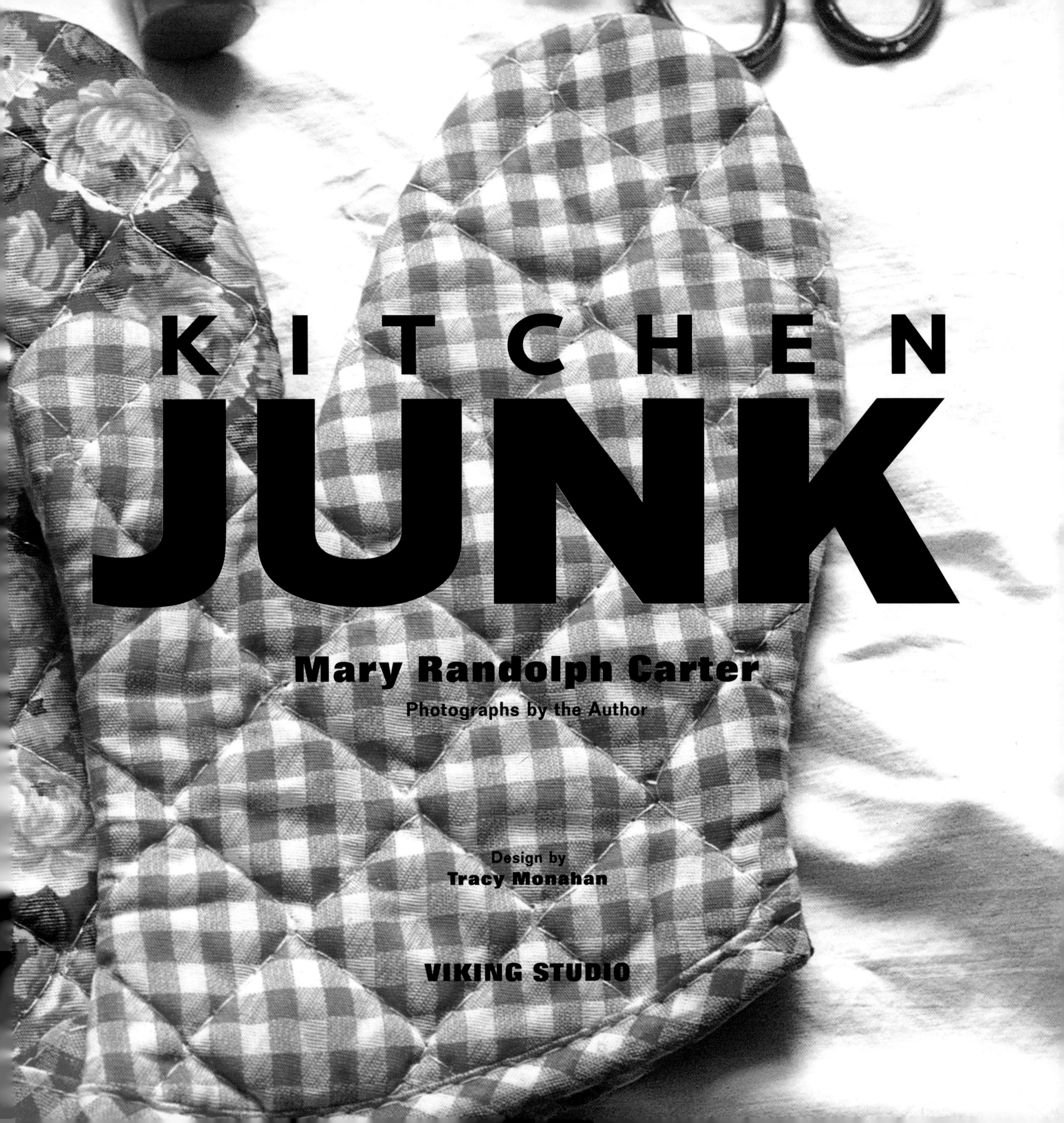

KITCHEN
JUNK

Mary Randolph Carter

Photographs by the Author

Design by
Tracy Monahan

VIKING STUDIO

VIKING STUDIO
Published by the Penguin Group
Penguin Putnam Inc., 375 Hudson Street,
New York, New York 10014, U.S.A.
Penguin Books Ltd, 27 Wrights Lane,
London W8 5TZ, England
Penguin Books Australia Ltd, Ringwood,
Victoria, Australia
Penguin Books Canada Ltd, 10 Alcorn Avenue,
Toronto, Ontario, Canada M4V 3B2
Penguin Books (N.Z.) Ltd, 182-190 Wairau Road,
Auckland 10, New Zealand

Penguin Books Ltd, Registered Offices:
Harmondsworth, Middlesex, England

First published in 1999 by Viking Studio,
a member of Penguin Putnam Inc.

1 3 5 7 9 10 8 6 4 2

Library of Congress Cataloging-in-Publication Data

Carter, Mary Randolph.
Kitchen Junk / Mary Randolph Carter; photographs by the author; design by Tracy Monahan.
p. cm.
ISBN 0-670-88099-X
1. Kitchens. 2. Secondhand trade. I. Title.
TX653.C35   1999
643' .3—dc21   98–53227

Printed in China
Set in Folio and Foundry
Designed by Tracy Monahan

For Howard

I started writing,
you started cooking.
I grew piles of junk,
you grew tomatoes.
My kitchen/your kitchen.

CONTENTS

ACKNOWLEDGMENTS

Kitchen Junk is the third book in my junk series. That makes it a junk triology. I like the way that sounds, but the junk quartet sounds even more exotic. By the time this book is in your hands I will probaby have begun yet another junk journey along slightly different junk topography.

The fuel for each of these books was supplied by many, but it's my family— my husband, my sons, my mother and father, my six sisters and two brothers and their families—that

My junker's jewels dangling from a necklace created especially for me by fellow junker and artist Nannette Pyron from Pullman, Washington. I wouldn't trade it for diamonds!

Samantha Warner-Garrick, Stephen Drucker, Carol Levison, Jerry Pontes, John Halpern, Bobby Ball, Sam Hamilton, and Lisa Durfee.

Abby Zabar and Alice Reid, one a neighbor in the city, the other in the country, both lent their kitchen wisdom to *Kitchen Junk*. Thank you, Alice and Abby.

Gloria Landers has been a stalwart supporter of my junking efforts since the very beginning. In

continues to sustain and inspire me. Their homes, lives, and this time their kitchens reveal a way of living that is unpretentious, unexpected, and all their own.

No one supports me more than my husband, Howard, to whom this book is dedicated. He, not kitchen junk (as I propose in the introduction), is the real spice of my life! My older son Carter assisted me often in the photography of this book, and took a real courageous leap in taking his mother's author portrait seen on the back flap. Thanks to my son Sam, who took great pains to convince me that I could not write another book on a typewriter. His determination and thoughtful lessons on his computer have rewarded me with a big step into the modern age. The only thing I miss is ripping out the paper from the typewriter, balling it up, and heaving it across the room.

The spirit of kitchen junk is defined by the creators and inhabitants of the kitchens you'll visit in the chapters to come. Special thanks to their owners: Ellen O'Neill, Mark Campbell, Laurie, Eddie, and

Kitchen Junk she has outdone herself with an astonishing exhibition of old recycled plastic kitchen tools—spatulas, spoons, cake knives, and the like. Thank you, Gloria.

A Sunday in the country is not the same without a visit to Laurie Higgins's Rummage Shoppe in Millerton, New York. It is an institution that has been a resource for all my junk books, but the mother lode for *Kitchen Junk*. Thank you, Laurie, for your great resourcefulness, and the real pleasure you give all of us Sunday addicts who know when all else fails you'll be there with the right stuff and a big smile.

Mike Fallon's Copake Auction in Copake, New York, has supplied me with many a good night of bidding among the best of them for some of my most-loved stuff. Mike has a big family, a big heart, and is totally nuts (a prerequisite for doing what he does!). Not only have he and his son Seth (now his partner in crime) awarded me some of my great auction moments, but they've also helped me find a way to get it all safely stored in my pickup. Thank you, Copake Auction family and friends.

When on the Outer Banks of North Carolina, I head to Jerry Pontes's Twisted Fish Gallery, Charles Reber's seaside workshop, The Merry-Go-Round Thrift Shop, and Jo Ruth Patterson's The Twila Zone. For years and years—almost two decades—these have been my friends and resources. Good friends and good junk endure!

Bobby and Vivian Leigh's Penny Paid is one of my favorite junking haunts in all of Virginia. Bobby's mother's mushroom clock seen on page 23 was a treasure buried on a back wall. Wow! Thanks, y'all. Down the road, and across the Rappahannock River in White Stone, Virginia, a high school basketball teammate of mine, Pat Lawson Kyzer, opened and recently closed Pat's Attic Treasures. She had a special passion for kitchen junk that coincided with my special hunt. The other good news is from time to time Pat minds American Junk, the junk emporium my sister Nell and I birthed on the Fourth of July 1997. Time out for a special thanks to Nellita, and all my family who contributed their time and junk to this noble establishment. Especially, Cleiland, Pat, Cary, Holly, and Dave. And special thanks to Betsy Crowther for all her help in answering calls and lugging books and faxes!

Ralph Lauren wrote the foreword to my first book, *American Family Style*, ten years ago. Soon after, I joined his family at Polo Ralph Lauren. Thank you, Ralph, for your warm support and the opportunity to watch at close range your vision, which is always unpredictable, very personal, real, smart, and truly original.

On my last birthday (who's counting?) my Polo family threw a great kitchen junk surprise birthday party for me. Some of their efforts you'll see in the pages ahead. Thank you, gang. And thank you, Susan Stevens, my special assistant and special supporter on all fronts. Although I have plenty of sisters, I've added another, Buffy Birritella, my close friend, junker-at-arms, and cohort for a decade at Polo.

It is the tenth anniversary of *American Family Style*, my first book published by Viking Studio. Michael Fragnito is the man who committed to its publication then and in the years following has stood behind the publication of *The Welcome Book*, *American Junk*, *Garden Junk*, and now *Kitchen Junk*. He has been my anchor in the turbulent word of publishing, and a believer in the dreams that I dream. Thank you, Michael.

Cheers to the rest of my Viking Studio team. To my new editor, Rachel Tsutsumi, may this be the first of many adventures to come. To Laura Healy for once again checking in with all my junkers across America so the Junk Guide can be a real roadmap for the readers of this book. To Ellen Gilinsky for putting all the pieces of this wild and crazy junking experience together, and making it into Junk Book III!

I found Steve Axelrod, my agent, more than ten years ago. He believed in family and helped me turn it into a book. He believed in junk and now it's a triology. Thank you, Steve. Onward!

On the road to *Garden Junk* and now *Kitchen Junk*, Tracy Monahan has been my constant visual navigator. Her contribution extends far beyond art direction. Her wit, intelligence, and total loyalty to junk has contributed far beyond what the eye can see. Around that corner, T., what do you see? More junk? Treasures for you and me? The journey continues . . .

Though Sam Landers was my husband's best friend since college, he became mine also. We started junking together three decades ago in Georgia, Florida, North Carolina, and upstate New York. Almost once a week I'd catch him at the tail end of a nightly chat with Howard. The conversation always turned to junk, my latest junk book, and the treasures we'd tracked down since our last talk. Years ago, I started calling Sam "Sam the Lion," after a character in *The Last Picture Show* that reminded me so much of him. He liked that. "The Lion" died suddenly last April, just two days before his birthday. Sometimes, since then, when I am out in the fields of junk I sense his presence, shaking his head, laughing at the silly thing I've just gone for, and loving it. I miss you, Sam the Lion.

The broom is of the cheap thirty- to forty-cent kind and is nearly new, but do not be misled: the old one, still held in limbo because nothing is thrown away, was well used before it was discarded. It has about the sweeping power of a club foot.

—James Agee
Let Us Now Praise Famous Men

kitchen junk: the spice of life

I can hardly grasp the memory of our kitchen in the big brick house set back on Monument Avenue in Richmond, Virginia. I know I ate my first bowl of cream of wheat there and probably tasted my first spoonful of creamed chipped beef. I seem to recall a brick floor and a large window over the sink that faced the backyard. If I crawled up on a stool, I could see the little blue playhouse with the red roof that protected a play kitchen, which I remember much better. We had a plywood stove with painted-on burners and a full set of miniature aluminum cookware. My sisters Cary and Nell and I would make the muddiest mud pies for our little brother, Jimmie. I think he actually ate one. We had two other kitchens in Richmond, and then we moved permanently into what had been our summer barn/house on the Rappahannock River in the Northern Neck of Virginia. My main memory of that kitchen was the winter before its renovation, when we would pull our chairs close to a huge old brown heater stove to stay warm as we ate our cereal before the school bus arrived. Sitting around that stove was like sitting around a big wooden table. When we eventually moved up the road to Muskettoe Pointe Farm, a seventeenth-century farmhouse, I was seventeen, and the family number had totaled in at eleven: my mother and father, seven girls, and two boys. Our kitchen table was an old picnic table we had dragged in from outdoors one summer and never returned. It sat in front of a huge fireplace, replacing that old brown stove at River Barn.

Left: The table in our farmhouse kitchen in the country is about the same size as the one that dominates our much smaller city kitchen, seen on the following page. It functions mostly as a worktable for mixing and chopping, but sometimes as a resting place for coffee for one. I love the wrecked green and mustard paint and and the number 1 painted on the left corner. Perhaps it was a homemade game table before I won it on a lucky (very low $10) bid at the Copake Auction in upstate New York. The little metal stool, a $5 pick-me-up at The Rummage Shoppe, Millerton, New York, and a cousin to Ellen O'Neill's, seen on page 128, will prop you up for a quick coffee break, but pass on it for dinner. The wooden bowl filled with crunchy Macouns was handmade in Trinidad and given to our family by Una Michaud, who lovingly ruled our kitchens, our lives, and our hearts forever and ever.

1

The kitchen my children will remember is the only one they have known (except our kitchen in the country) since they were each born. It is twelve stories up, with a window next to the stove that looks out on the rooftops of a myriad of venerable old New York brownstones, the backside of a 1940s high-rise facing Fifth Avenue, and a view of the treetops of Central Park seen over the skylight roof of the Metropolitan Museum. In the center of this 11' x 11' space is a little primitive wooden table with a top that measures 22" x 45". I bought it almost twenty-five years ago in a little antique shop in the Village. When the top started to get too splintery, I tacked on a cover of red-and-white-checked oilcloth. The old square-headed nails still pop up through the little checks and sometimes snag our clothes. When the four of us sit at the table, it's a tight squeeze, but once in place we rarely have to rise because everything is at our fingertips. The refrigerator door is an arm's length away (my tall sons have very long arms!); so are the top of the stove, the water faucet and the sink, the open shelves that store our glasses and plates, the old toolbox that separates forks, spoons, and knives. We can squeeze in one easygoing guest or a couple of medium-size children, but no more than that. Sometimes in the summer on a very hot night we pick up the table and carry it into our cooler hallway dining room.

Right: A sliver of the kitchen my children grew up in. It is anchored by the oilcloth-covered table in the foreground and surrounded by souvenirs of their childhood interspersed with more serviceable things. (See more of it on the endpapers at the front and back of the book.)

Above, clockwise from top left: 1. Stephen Drucker's really big kitchen calendar, compliments of the *East Hampton Star* newspaper, on Long Island. **2.** Star time in the kitchen: an old Texaco gas station star floating over a 3-D ceramic plaque of rock 'n' roll's star and king Elvis the Pelvis! The metal sign commemorates the old Texaco station in White Stone, Virginia, which now houses our American Junk store, pumping out junk every weekend. (Check the Junk Guide for more info.) Having presided over many a meeting of the White Stone chapter of the Elvis Presley fan club (I was the founder and president in seventh grade), former classmate and collector Patsy Lawson Kyzer made sure I didn't leave her store without my idol in tow. **3.** A miniature scrubbing board illustrated with a delectable menu of hand washables hangs on our kitchen wall as utility art. **4.** A feast of fish platters, plates, and mugs specially created for me by potter Sandy Aldrich and given to me on birthdays and anniversaries by my husband Howard. They are stored in our country kitchen in a plate rack made by my father. The little blue-and-white boat, picking up on the nautical theme, was made by Outer Banks artist Charles Reber. **5.** The communications center and scrapbook of the home, the refrigerator. (See more on page 190.)

More living gets done in the kitchen than any other room of the house. It's the source of nourishment (all kinds), dialogue, camaraderie, thanksgiving, information (more morning newspapers get read in the kitchen than any other room), and planning. What would a kitchen be without the kitchen calendar? Where do you leave a note for a member of the family if you're dashing out? The kitchen really is the communications command post of the home, and because it is also the real living room, it tends to collect stuff. The refrigerator becomes a bulletin board for not only children's artwork but Little League schedules, wedding invitations, quotes (see three-year-old Samantha Warner-Garrick's icebox art show on page 94 and ours at left). The kitchen is a three-dimensional home scrapbook. We not only decorate it with the things that we need—the shelves stacked and lined with plates and cups, glassware, spice boxes, canisters and cookbooks, pots and pans strung from ceiling racks, wooden spoons, spatulas, mashers, choppers, graters, slicers, rolling pins, and whisks stuck into odd jars, bins, and baskets—but also with the things that we don't necessarily need but want to have around us: sentimental kitchen samplers, old enamel coffeepots way past their prime, odd pitchers, mismatched ironstone plates, novelty coffee cups, the weirdest salt and pepper shakers, every chicken and rooster collectible, ceramic corncobs, vintage flyswatters, old-fashioned aprons, a string of keys that will never unlock another lock, but may unlock your heart.

I always seem to be confessing what I am not and what my junk books (*American Junk*, 1994, and *Garden Junk*, 1997) are. Ready for this one? I am not a great cook, but I do love my kitchens (city and country) and all the make-believe ones I've conjured up in *Kitchen Junk*: "Matador's Breakfast," inspired by my love of Hemingway and Pamplona; a kitchen totally decorated with red and white checks in "A Checkered Life"; and my ode to chicken and rooster junk celebrated in an old wooden chicken coop in upstate New York. *Kitchen Junk* is more about the stuff and dreams of kitchens than about kitchens themselves. Sometimes that means trailing an old stove to South Central Los Angeles, as Stephen Drucker did. Or understanding why Ellen O'Neill has filled her dream kitchen with things that she will never use, like her favorite, very serviceable green dust-pan that hangs on a nail on the wall collecting dust! Or how the discovery of an old faded green graniteware roasting pan inspired Bobby Ball to redo totally his cozy country kitchen in Virginia. *Kitchen Junk* is also about good housekeeping the way it used to be done. It's about wooden cows and plastic picnics, setting tables like impressionistic paintings, cooking on a wooden stove, trading in Starbucks for cowboy coffee, inviting Frida Kahlo for lunch and Ernest Hemingway for breakfast. *Kitchen Junk* is about journeys from the kitchens of our childhood, the kitchens of another era, of another country—to creating the kitchen of our hearts.

A table set for a junker's sweet tooth with a cupcake teapot, $3, a strawberry sugar dish, $2, and a pineapple compote, $5, all handcrafted and served up at the SoHo Flea Market, New York City.

ROAD TRIPS

Michael and Seth Fallon, father and son, and partners in Copake Auction in Copake, New York, are veteran journeymen. Take a look at their truck, seen above, packed like a work of art. They are the Houdinis of packing and unpacking stuff! What they do is beyond most of us (can you imagine taking that rig out on the highway?), but here are some packing tips from the master mavens of moving.

- Pack tight and right the first time.
- The load always shifts forward, especially during an emergency stop.
- Heavy items go on the bottom.
- Don't rewrite *Gone With the Wind*. Face drawers in; keep doors and lids away from airflow.
- Use every space available, especially the inside of drawers, cupboards, and blanket boxes or trunks.
- Insulate! Rubbing surfaces kill finishes. Packing blankets are great, but you can use available materials, including cardboard, quilts, rugs, etc.
- The right stuff: Bungees have a tendency to break. Use polypropylene rope. It's impervious to climate and you can untie it and reuse.
- Clearance: With a load more than 10 feet high, you had better know where you are going. Cable and phone lines are easy to bring down.
- Be creative. Sometimes removing legs from a table will save you from a return trip.
- Most important: be safe!

JUNKER'S ETIQUETTE: PLEASE HAGGLE!

Let's make a deal is the name of the game. Most dealers worth their junk expect a bit of a tug-of-war. Go lower, and you'll end up somewhere in the middle. Don't insult a dealer with a muttered under-the-breath "I can't believe these prices." Be nice. Be honest, and if there's more than one thing you're interested in, deal for the lot, not individual items. I recently haggled and lost, thanked the gentleman, and started to depart. He called me back and made the deal.

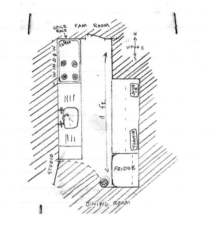

RECIPE FOR A JUNK KITCHEN

Lisa Durfee's Kitchen Recipe, seen above, with a little penciled floor plan of her kitchen in upstate New York (see pages 146-49), says it all—"Stuff with Junk." No matter how small (many of the kitchens you're about to meet *are* small) or large (lucky you!), old or new your kitchen is, there is room not only for cooking and eating but for creating a space that is lively and fun.

TEAM SPIRIT:
HOW TO KEEP IT GOING WITH CHILDREN (OF ALL AGES!)

If you're foraging with friends and family, as I was last year at the Long Beach Outdoor Market in California (with Lucinda Chambers, the fashion director of *British Vogue* on my right, and Laurie, Eddie, and Samantha Warner-Garrick on my left), establish some ground rules before you take off.

- Pick a spot where to meet if lost and a place to meet (if you're not) at a designated time.
- Don't count on finding the best food at flea market prices. We brought a picnic of our own and lots of water and juices.
- Though four-year-old Samantha is a veteran junker, her parents have learned how to make it an experience she looks forward to. 1. She has her own little junk bag with her favorite juice inside and her junking fund of $1. 2. Mom and Dad take turns junking with Sam because when you junk with a young junker, you have to focus almost entirely on her search.
- Choose a junking buddy who has the same pace as you do, but possibly not the same taste. Or go it alone (at large flea markets this tends to happen anyway) and meet up later.
- At the end of the hunt, share what you've found with your friends. Try not to be jealous if they got something you would have died for. Find out what they spent and offer them a better price . . . just kidding!

NEVER LEAVE HOME WITHOUT IT: THE LIST

Before I took off for a junking journey in Sonoma last year, I faxed my friend Jann Johnson a list of all the places I wanted to explore. She faxed back a grid guide (see right) to days and times. It became our crumpled compass.

The other list you need is like the one you write out before you go to the grocery store. My kitchen junk list read like my grocery store version: milk bottles, egg crates, chickens. See how successful I was in the chapters ahead.

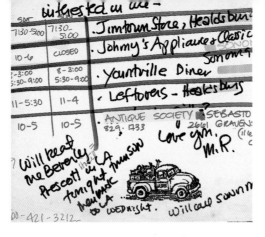

NEVER STOP TO THINK, "DO I HAVE A PLACE FOR THIS?"

DEAR DIARY

Call it a junk diary, journal, notebook, or ledger. It's a place to record what you bought, where you bought it, when, and how much. I kept eight volumes for this book alone. See volume above. I drag my Polaroid along to celebrate the moment and save the treasure in all its naked glory (see a moment top right) before I get it home or truck it down to American Junk. I save the dealer's card when possible and scrawl down anything in particular that endeared me to adopt the homeless skillet, stove, dinette set, coffee cup, or dustpan that's from that moment recorded in my junk annals and officially part of my life.

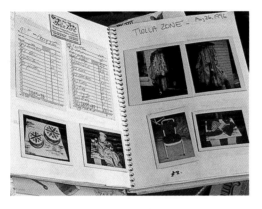

DRESS CODE

Toe to head dress comfortably. Start with comfortable shoes. My old shoelaceless blue sneakers have seen a long tour of duty. Now that the toes have worn out, they're air-conditioned! Don't wear sandals; you're likely to drop something on your bare feet, plus fields of junk are dusty. Boots, unless they're extremely comfortable, tend to be heavy and hot. If it's raining, go for it. Protect your head with a lightweight cap with a brim. I can't seem to give up my weathered captain's cap, seen top right and on the opposite page. It's unconstructed and light and covers my nose. Dress in layers. Part of my junker's camouflage is a fishing vest. Each pocket serves a purpose.

BE PREPARED

An inventory of my junker's vest, pocket by pocket:

- Cash in small denominations. Most dealers will take checks with the right I.D.—i.e., a driver's license—but who wants to write a check for $5?

- Notebook and pen to record finds (see "Dear Diary").

- Wash'n Dri towelettes to wipe off the junky grime. Porta Pottis don't come with sinks and rarely with toilet paper, so carry a wad of tissues too.

- A small magnifying glass to check out the fine print, cracks, marks, and "Made in Japan" on the bottom.

- A Polaroid or disposable camera if you want to savor every moment.

Along with the fishing vest, I carry one of those big and sturdy plastic shopping bags with the double handles (see page 21) to stow a million little purchases. Real veterans out for the big stuff bring their own shopping carts or wagons, but most large flea markets usually have them at least to get you to your vehicle.

a checkered life

Clockwise from top left: 1. An invisible hand spoons raspberry sauce onto a scoop of vanilla ice cream nesting on crisply toasted waffles. This absurd plastic sculpture, a loan from Alice Reid's weirdo kitchen art collection, was, according to Alice, a gift shop item popular in the 1970s. She got it and another—a suspended carton pouring a stream of milk onto a bowl of cereal—from an auction for about $20. She estimates its original worth at about $30. The tartan plastic plate was one of a set of four manufactured by Ornamin and discovered for 40 cents each at The Rummage Shoppe, Millerton, New York. The Flagmaid raspberry jam jelly jar directly behind it, and seen on page 12, was salvaged as cheap glassware in the 1950s and recently bought at Northeast Antiques, Millerton, New York, for 75 cents each. The white glass hen nest (more on hen nests on pages 117 and 121) to its right was a prize found at a moving sale five minutes from my front door in upstate New York, for $4. **2.** A major coffee cup and saucer broadcasting the owner's status as Mom was not easy to overlook or leave behind at Kitty Hawk Thrift & Consignment, Kitty Hawk, North Carolina. The major price to consider was $10.50. **3.** The calico rooster, the centerpiece of the table on page 9, was the predominant kitchen motif from the 1940s to the 1960s. It strutted its stuff on everything from kitchen towels to pottery plates. (Check out the wooden canisters on page 60.) This proud beauty was plucked from a shelf of stuff at The Consignment Shop, Locust Hill, Virginia, for $4. **4.** The windmill potholder holder was a West Coast find at Cookin', San Francisco, for $16. The quilted oven mitts were a triple score at Penny Paid, Locust Hill, Virginia, for a quarter apiece. **5.** A 12-ounce Ritz cracker can from Americana Collectibles, in Hudson, New York. (See "Tin Pan Alley," page 181 for more history.) **6.** A housewife's sentiments, probably from the 1950s, cross-stitched with pride. My proud find for $4.50, at Merry-Go-Round Thrift Shop, Kill Devil Hills, North Carolina. **7.** A very resourceful handyperson (not I!) recharged the life of a waning match safe with a new wardrobe of red-and-white-checked contact paper. The cost was $2, at D's Place, Gloucester, Virginia. See it in its red-and-white-checked context on page 20.

I've always associated red-and-white-checked things—tablecloths, napkins, dish towels, and aprons—with the kitchen. For as long as I can remember, the top of our little wooden table in the kitchen (see page 2) has been tacked over with a piece of red-and-white-checked oilcloth. Before that it was covered with a red-and-white-checked tablecloth—the kind you associate, but rarely see anymore, with diners. Historically gingham was the cheapest, hardiest cotton fabric woven into checks, plaids, or stripes. It was sold in bolts at the Wal-Mart of early Americans, the general store. The housewife traveled miles in her wagon to carry back neat yards of it folded and wrapped in brown paper packages. Those red-and-white checks were the warm welcome in her windows, on her table, and the fabric of the apron she tied around her waist. It was my discovery, in one day, of a red-and-white-checked match safe, candy tin, and cookbook (see page 20) that inspired my journey into the sometimes wacky kitchen world of red-and-white checks.

Preceding pages: Set for breakfast, a 1930s enamel-porcelain drop leaf table (with slide-under extensions) decorated with red stencil designs, red-and-white-checked paper place mats (from a local diner), jelly jar glasses, a red bandanna rooster, and nesting hens. The table for $40, and four red chairs for $20, were bargains from Alice Reid's Antiques in the Barn, Livingston, New York.

Above: Instead of a canvas, the artist who created Pie-Ala-Mode—a kitchen masterpiece found for $22 at The Garage, New York City—used an old porcelain-enamel tabletop. How many times have you found a wobbly old table with a good enamel top? Next time buy it, use the base for kindling, and start your own work of art.

Growing up in a large family—seven girls, two boys—each person had specific chores of the kitchen. Because there were so many of us, we were able to make some choices based on our particular abilities. What I enjoyed, and still do, was creating atmosphere, which meant that I got to set the table. The table seen at right and on pages 8-9 is not exactly the table I would have set as a child, but it is a table built on the fantasy of the farmyard in all versions of red and white. Best of all, it satisfies a child's yearnings to bring her toys to the table.

Right: More pie-in-the-sky table dressing: a faux cherry pie served up on a plastic plate, resting on the real work of art, a crocheted doily recovered for $2 from a table of vintage handiwork at the Long Beach Outdoor Market in California. The milk glass hen nesting behind it was $7 from a local tag sale. The china one, to its left, saddled with a pair of salt and pepper shakers, was $10, from the same sale. The towering milk bottle, on loan from friend and collector Lisa Durfee (more about her collections on pages 146-49), was a hand-me-down from her father's kitchen in New York City.

12

Above: Mark Campbell's blue and graniteware pitcher matches his collection of bowls seen on page 53. It cost him only $5 at the Twenty-sixth Street Flea Market (or, as Mark refers to it, the Flea), New York City, but that's because there's a hole in it. No problem—Mark hides an old bottle inside and uses it as a striking country vase. The enameled metal bread box (more on bread bins on pages 178-79) was $15, also at the Flea.

Right: Four white graniteware pitchers lined up against a backdrop of red-and-white stripes just outside Mark Campbell's summer kitchen (see more of Mark's starting on page 48). Though these probably date back to the turn of the century, they have a timeless and almost modern look to them. From left to right they were $4, $8, $6, and $6 at the Flea. There is hardly a Saturday or Sunday you won't see Mark there. Go early or go late. See hours and general information in the Junk Guide at the back of the book.

14

A sampler of red-and-white checks and ginghams sewed and crocheted into all manner of serviceable cloths for the kitchen. Tablecloths, place mats, and potholders picked up from coast to coast for $2 to 10 cents. A great way to display your collection is on an old wooden drying rack. This one was rummaged, from Fredie's Shack, Geneva, New York, for $10. (Check Lisa Durfee's laundering tips for aprons on page 37.)

AT YOUR SERVICE: GINGHAMS, STRIPES, AND CHECKS

My loyalty to red-and-white stripes and checks in the kitchen has little to do with their utilitarian history. I've just always loved my piles of red-and-white-checked cloth napkins, dish towels, and gingham tablecloths. The workhorse history of gingham has only recently intrigued me. I pass it along to you with the assurance that sometimes your heart can tell you to love something for no particular reason, and later your head informs you that no matter how silly you felt, you did the right thing. I loved gingham because it was simple, cheap, and cheerful. The first ginghams were imported from India and were made of cotton and silk. Woven of multiple-stranded warps and wefts, it was noted for its toughness of texture. Its American incarnation was purely cotton woven with dyed yarns often in stripes and checks. By the mid-nineteenth century it was well established as an American staple, manufactured to a large extent in the fabric mills of Massachusetts. A true gingham has equal-width stripes in both directions of the weave and is woven only from two colors, with the threads set up in such a way that a third color is formed where the two colors meet. Vegetable dyes of deep indigo, greens, and reds were the original favorites and remain so today. In a 1930s issue of a Sears, Roebuck & Company catalog, there are two whole pages devoted to "Serviceable Fabrics" largely featuring ginghams. There are superior ginghams for dresses at 27 cents a yard and apron ginghams for 13 cents a yard. Today's ginghams cost about $6 a yard. Search and you will find all manner of ginghams—in aprons, oven mitts, napkins, curtains, dish towels, tablecloths, and even cookbook covers (as seen on the following page). Fall in love with gingham. There's enough out there for all of us.

I started collecting cookbooks almost twenty years ago, when a good friend gave me *The Virginia Housewife* by Mary Randolph. The author, no relation, published in 1860 not only her "receipts" with their proper weights and measures but also advice to the young housewife on household management: "Early rising is also essential to the good government of a family. A late breakfast deranges the whole business of the day, and throws a portion of it of the next, which opens the door for confusion to enter." *Bull Cook and Authentic Historical Recipes and Practices*, by George Leonard Herter and Berthe E. Herter, must be the cult book of the cooking world. First published in 1960, it contains the very erudite ramblings of George Herter on everything from English Roast Beef to "How to Clean Catfish and Bullheads" to helpful hints on "How to Survive in the Wilderness in Case of a Hydrogen Bomb Attack." I only recently acquired the hard-to-find volumes 2 and 3 through book searcher friend Howard Frisch located in Livingston, New York (see Junk Guide). Another great source for vintage cookbooks is Kitchen Arts and Letters in New York City. Almost any secondhand bookstore, like one of my favorites, Rodgers Book Barn in Hillsdale, New York, has big sections of cookbooks. Whether you use them as a recipe resource or, like me, to fill your kitchen bookshelves with red-and-white checks, they're an easy, inexpensive, and often fascinating journey into the minds of the cooks and housewives who preceded us.

Learning To Cook Book

NEW YORK STATE ELECTRIC & GAS
CORPORATION

Above left: *Good Meals and How to Prepare Them*, published in 1929 by the Good Housekeeping Institute, offered its readers not only a guide to meal planning, cooking, and serving but a serviceable ginghamlike checked cover that could be, according to its instructions, wiped off lightly with a damp cloth to remove soil; readers were warned not to rub it with soapy water or an abrasive. Originally free to subscribers of *Good Housekeeping* (two years for $4.50), it cost me $1.25, at Rodgers Book Barn, Hillsdale, New York.

Above right: Hooked again on the red-and-white checks and the fetching aproned housewife (so happy with her steaming meal) adorning the cover of *The Home Menu Cook Book* (1934), I immediately added it to my collection for $3.50, from Way Back When, Canaan, Connecticut. The wooden-handled pickle fork/can opener (de rigueur for any respectable bar or kitchen of the 1940s and 1950s) is carved like a Campbell soup kid with a red-and-white polka-dotted dunce hat. A happy find at The Carriage Factory Antique Center, Flint, New York, for $2.

Opposite: Cooking pamphlets are a great source of kitchen and cooking fun. Many were published by food manufacturers as goodwill promotions for their products. The Home Service Department of the New York State Electric & Gas Corporation put out this helpful booklet for young cooks and their moms. Table etiquette was slipped in as "A Badge of Good Manners." Some of the golden tips passed along: "Take small bites of food...chew and swallow quietly. Sit straight in your chair...do not lean on the table or annoy the people around you." I secured this little beauty for 50 cents at The Second Hand Shop in Geneva, New York. Main attraction: the ponytailed young homemaker sketched on the cover. Her hairdo suggests the 1950s, the age of home economics.

Taking a curtain call at center stage right is Mrs. Butterworth, unburdened of her syrupy load and transformed to a star of the kitchen in a bright new wardrobe, the painterly handiwork of some unknown wardrobe mistress. It's a loan from Lisa Durfee, a collector and dealer who swept her out of oblivion at the Salvation Army Thrift Store, Danbury, Connecticut, for $1.50. The miniature stage set, presented on the top of a wobbly, weathered kitchen table (seen in full on the opposite page), is the grand finale of my red-and-white-checked foraging expeditions. On top of one of the paper diner mats previously seen on page 10, sits our circular red-and-white-checked cookie tin stage, which was 50 cents from Merry-Go-Round Thrift Shop, Kill Devil Hills, North Carolina. To its right is a full view of the pickle poker seen on the previous page and a little red-and-white-checked note pad to hold Mrs. Butterworth's script notes, 10 cents from a tag sale box lot. To its left is a red Dutch Girl cleanser shaker, seen again on page 61. The child's toy iron is a coming attraction from the next chapter, seen on page 27. The lean-to of cookbooks, previously explored on page 19, sits under the match safe introduced on page 10. A full shot of the kitchen clock perched over my favorite sampler, $30 from Madalin, Tivoli, New York, is seen on page 196. In place of footlights lies a plastic red-and-white spatula, 30 cents from The Rummage Shoppe, Millerton, New York.

Clockwise from top left: 1. If I had been the costume designer for *The Wizard of Oz*, then Dorothy's shoes would have been red-and-white checks like the ones I found on a rainy Fourth of July two years ago at Madalin in Tivoli, New York, for $8. Charley, my son Carter's black Labrador, liked them too. Note the chunk missing out of the front of the right shoe! **2.** Looks like a little girl's Sunday best. Wrong! It's a clothespin bag to hang on a hanger and then on the line. Another Fourth of July find from Madalin for $12. **3.** When not transporting groceries or laundry from store to home, from upstairs to laundry room, from city to country, from beach to city, this roomy Mexican tote could be used for a very big game of checkers. How it ended up in western New York in The Second Hand Shop in Geneva is one of those unsolved junk mysteries. How about the owner picked it up on a warm vacation away from the snowy Finger Lakes district— say, in Mexico—and one day decided to ditch it at the local thrift? Sound good? Very good to me since I picked it up to tote my newfound junk in for $3. No mystery there. (New ones can be found at American Junk, White Stone, Virginia, from $8 to $15.)

21

Our New York City kitchen measures 11' x 11.' To the four of us who have cooked, eaten, and lived in it for twenty-four years it seems just the right size. A lot of that has to do with the comfort of returning day after day to a place that is known. Sitting at a familiar table, surrounded by walls of shelves supporting stacks of ironstone plates, yellowware mixing bowls, cookbooks, photographs, paintings, eclectic pottery, molds, ladles, wooden spoons, children's artwork, a star-shaped souvenir of Elvis, an old Texaco gas station sign, two sets of green shutters, and an indispensable banana clipboard that holds all those important phone numbers, schedules, invitations, and menus for ordering in. The wall at right demonstrates the same kind of ingenuity and space management and, yes, the frivolity one needs to apply in a small kitchen area. Hang chairs on the wall (the Shakers did); hang an apron on the chair, a knife rack next to a kitchen masterpiece like the bacon and eggs still life hinted at here and seen in full on the opposite page. And if you have a big kitchen, even better. Things on the wall, sensible as well as senseless, foster utility, coziness, and a creative context to one of our simplest pleasures: sharing a meal.

NO MORE STARBUCKS, IT'S COWBOY COFFEE TIME!

A real home-on-the-range cowboy would take his cleanest sock, fill it with coffee grounds, knot it, throw it into his kettle, and boil it off for four or five minutes. Diehards drink their coffee strong and black. They wouldn't be toting a quart of milk around and they'd save the sugar.

Opposite: Kitchen utility and frivolity expressed in a corner of my make-believe checkered fantasy. From left to right: A wooden knife rack with floral decal was $14 from Madalin, Tivoli, New York; a plastic bib apron (modeled on yours truly on page 34) was lent by Lisa Durfee, who added it to her extensive apron collection for 25 cents; the polka-dotted folding chair was one of a set of four that was found years ago at a tag sale in Hillsdale, New York, for $2; the red-and-white kitchen stool was wheeled out of the back bargain room of The Twila Zone, Nags Head, North Carolina, for $8; the graniteware kettle, actually known as a coffee boiler, another tag sale find for $5, is the perfect vessel for making cowboy coffee (see recipe on the opposite page). Framing the right side of the page is a plastic curtain panel printed with farmyard scenics, kitchen gold dug up at Madalin, for $20.

Top left: The mushroom clock telling time in my checkered kitchen had a checkered life all its own way before it came into mine. I discovered it at Penny Paid, one of my favorite stops near my family's home in Virginia. Bobby Lee, the coowner, closed the deal for $4, then revealed it was his mother's. Her kitchen was a mushroom theme park decorated with all forms of the famous fungi. He pointed out other pieces: a pair of mushroom trivets, salt and pepper shakers, and a platter. I left with only the clock and visions of the elder Mrs. Lee's mushroom paradise. Perhaps it is up to me to carry on the tradition . . . one mushroom at a time.

Bottom left: Below the mushroom clock is hung the prize find of my kitchen collecting thus far, an oil painting of a hearty breakfast consisting of three fried eggs, sunny side up, a side of bacon, hash browns, a side order of toast, a cup of coffee, and possibly, in the upper left corner, a small bowl of cereal and bananas. The discovery was made at Thriftique, Millerton, New York, now a regular stop on my Saturday tour. It was hidden on a low shelf with a few other artworks, and when I uncovered it, I stifled a gasp. I wondered if the schoolchild's inspiration might have been breakfast at the Millerton Diner—just a few doors away.

good housekeeping

In 1919 Lydia Ray Balderston declared in *Housewifery*, that "every housewife ought to become as proficient in her realm as the businessman is in his. As a man cannot do good work without the best facilities and most careful organization in his office, so the housewife is handicapped unless her workshop is suitably planned and arranged." At the brink of the new millennium, Lydia Ray would undoubtedly prescribe a different course for good housekeeping, given the reality that most women have abandoned the home workshop for the work workshop. The tasks of good housekeeping–the cleaning, the laundry, the ironing–unfortunately have not disappeared, but they have (thank goodness!) become less tedious thanks to laborsaving technology and a home team that now encompasses more than one apron wearer. The indispensable tools of the housekeeper's trade have now become the prized collectibles of rummage shops, thrift stores, auctions, and tag sales. Old wooden ironing boards no longer groan under the burden of cast-iron sadirons. (Turn to page 28 and applaud the ingenuity of one collector who turned his into a handy sideboard.) Hefty irons double as doorstops. Iron trivets are put to work as durable bookends. Wooden clothespins, clothespin bags, and fanciful dish towels, like the Housewife's Crying Towel, seen on page 37, remind us of the housewife's daily dramas and tedious tasks. And aprons, once considered the uniform of the day, are now tied on as kitchen fashion by both men and women.

Above: A housekeeping vignette created out of the indispensable tools of the housewife's workplace–now relics of another time and state of mind.
Opposite: A collection of freshly washed vintage dish towels and tablecloths folded and ready for takeoff in a fold-up laundry basket, circa 1950, rolled out of the Long Beach Outdoor Market, California, held the third Sunday of every month (see Junk Guide for more information), for $15.

My make-believe laundry room set up in the loft of the barn at our farm in upstate New York. The ironing board in the foreground was $1 from the same auction where I got my cupboard. The laundry basket in pristine condition was scooped up from The Rummage Shoppe, Millerton, New York, for $3. The cutout wooden teapot attached to the inside of the cupboard door at right supports a wooden pineapple clipboard, which in turn supports a set of plastic bowl covers (they look like miniature shower caps for dolls), and an ashtray frying pan. The teapot-shaped potholder hanger was $12 from Madalin, Tivoli, New York. The kitchen clip and frying pan ashtray were 75 cents each at The Rummage Shoppe. The bowl covers were presented in their original packaging from my friend Gloria Landers. The apron decorated with kitchenalia and a turquoise waistband was $5 at Kitschen, New York City.

September 20, 1997: It's a Saturday night, and I'm at my favorite place—the Copake Auction—doing my favorite thing: bidding on the leftovers of other people's lives. I sit on the edge of my chair for five hours, clutching my number, 26, and propelling it above my head every time something stirs my imagination. When the cream-colored wainscoted cupboard, seen on the opposite page, is wheeled in, my heart catches. It's a huge hand-made two-piece storage masterpiece. When the auctioneer motions for the doors to be opened, the most heavenly old flowered wallpaper is revealed on the back walls and shelves. The bidding begins. When we pass $100, I feel an imaginary foot (mine) moving toward an imaginary brake (my budget!). My adversary screeches to a halt at the next bid. The cupboard is mine for $125.

Top: A convention of lilliputian toy irons and ironing boards collected randomly from $7 (the blue electric) to mostly $3 for the rest. The portable wooden sleeve ironer was $10 at Villa's Auction Gallery, Canaan, Connecticut.

Bottom left: The jovial bow-tied chef in charge of a burdensome list, traveled from D's Place at Holland's Stage Coach Markets, Gloucester, Virginia, for $4.

Bottom right: Before the invention of the sprinkler bottle, laundry was prepared for pressing by ironers dipping their fingers in water and flinging it over each piece. Although it's not known exactly when the sprinkler bottle was invented, it seems to have been around since the the mid-nineteenth century. Early ones were made of handblown clear glass or a metallike zinc. The most collectible are figural-shaped ceramic laundrymen, happy maids, elephants, and cats dating from the 1920s. The more utilitarian plastic milk bottle covered in orange netting and topped with a green sprinkler head was probably from the 1950s. I almost overlooked it at The Rummage Shoppe, Millerton, New York, for $1.25.

Above: A pair of iron holders have found new employment holding books. They were salvaged from a tag sale for $1 apiece.

My personal history of ironing dates to around my twelfth year. Between seven and seven-thirty on weekday mornings, my two younger sisters and I would rush to claim the iron and ironing board first. We each had a school bus to catch, and particularly in the warmer months, a blouse or skirt to dewrinkle. We'd set it up in the kitchen, and the first claimant was forced to iron to the fairly good-humored chidings of the other two. "Hurry up now. You'll make us all late." Comments like these were endured as well as could be expected but often impeded a respectable job. Scorches and wet splotches from an aggressive ironing speed were the result of many of these pressing exercises. I gave up ironing years ago. I prefer my cotton clothes and sheets smoothed by hand straight from the clothesline (my fantasy!) or out of the dryer. Why, then, do I take such pride in collecting and displaying the trophies of a task I relinquished long ago? Is it for the glory of ironing or irony?

John Halpern chose an old turkey farm in Bridgehampton, New York, as the perfect getaway. If getting away precludes ironing, why is there an ironing board set up in the middle of his living room? To hold sculptures, magazines, books of poetry, mail. When a yard-sale-collector-friend offered it to him, he never had any intention of burdening it with his unironed shirts or sheets. He didn't accept an ironing board; he received a splendid fold-up wooden table.

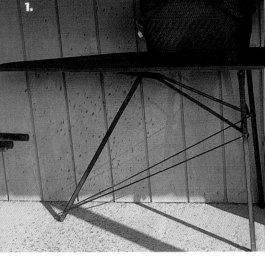

Clockwise from top left: 1. Ironing board or table, this beauty with green metal legs was $15 at Holland's Stage Coach Markets, Gloucester, Virginia. **2.** A mixed buffet of every kind of metal—from cast-iron sadirons to silver pitchers to a few rusty saws thrown in for flavor. This lavish spread is served up every weekend at the SoHo Flea Market at Grand Street and Broadway. (For more info, check the Junk Guide.) **3.** Perfect cargo for a wire fold-up laundry cart, seen previously on page 24: two toy ironing boards. The cart was $15; the pink board, $9; the pipsqueak, dented but irresistible with red legs to boot, $5. A triple strike for good housekeeping at the flea market in Long Beach, California. **4.** The standard size for an ironing board is 56 inches. Before the fold-up board was invented, a housekeeper would have to stretch a board between two chairs or a chair and a table. This wooden ironing board has legs, but in this naked condition it is better used as a table, like John Halpern's on pages 28–29. Or, clothe it in a comfy protective ironing board cover and let the tedious task begin! **5.** It was never too early to engage a young woman in the art of good housekeeping. For starters how about a perfectly scaled-down ironing board? This modern model is made for today's girls *and* boys.

Clockwise from top left: 1. A surreal surprise, an ironing board, dressed and ready to work, in a parking lot flea market in downtown Manhattan. **2.** In 1903 Earl Richardson invented an electric iron with a "hot point," launching the Hotpoint trade name in appliances. A year later General Electric presented an electric iron, but it was another thirty years before the electric iron became a mainstay because the use of electricity was so limited. In the market for a new iron? They do turn up at flea markets right alongside Pyrex coffeepots and cast-iron sadirons. The General Electric for sale in good condition was a bargain at $10. **3.** Proof of exactly how indispensable the electric iron became: the Handyhot Travel Iron. Manufactured in the 1950s, portable irons guaranteed a wrinkle-free holiday. The name and packaging were what seduced me for $5 at Fredie's Shack, Geneva, New York. The little iron on top is a not the Handyhot, but a toy iron picked up at Elephant's Trunk Bazaar, New Milford, Connecticut, for $11. It makes a great kitchen paperweight. **4.** A child's garden of earthly delights manifested on the top of a miniature metal ironing board, passed up for a few bucks at Holland's Stage Coach Markets, Gloucester, Virginia. **5.** The gasoline iron introduced in the 1930s was promoted with ads that told readers, "On ironing day just scratch a match, light your iron and in a few minutes you are ready to start ironing! No tramping from stove to ironing board, no hot stove to keep going." What no one mentioned was the threat of an explosion! A rare Coleman gas iron, finished in baby blue enamelware with a wooden handle, worth around $40 according to a recent kitchen collectibles price guide. It was priced at almost twice that at the Twenty-sixth Street Flea Market, New York City. Bye-bye.

Handyhot Travel IRON CAT. NO. 1178

Above: A little tin lunch box serves up not a peanut butter and jelly sandwich but a tasty supply of wooden clothespins.

In 1970 I bought a book of Andrew Wyeth's paintings and came upon his saved memory of a clothesline in a work titled *Slight Breeze*. Wyeth's romance with that moment and that clothesline has nothing to do with the drudgery of washdays before the invention of the washing machine and dryer. Drying yards chosen for their exposure to the sun and air were the necessary laundry rooms of the day. The clothespins stored in the deep pockets of the laundress's apron or the cargo of a colorful clothespin bag, like the one seen at right, were the essential links to the clothesline guaranteeing that no breeze—"slight" or otherwise—would release those washday trophies to the soil below.

Right: The reigning kingpin of this lively floral clothespin bag discovered filled with dozens of assorted pins in The Second Hand Shop, Geneva, New York, for $8, is actually a rubber squeeze toy from D's Place at Holland's Stage Coach Markets, Gloucester, Virginia. A princely prize for $5, his court consists of both push-on and spring-clip clothespins originally manufactured at the end of the nineteenth century and virtually unchanged today. Premanufacturing, the most prized pins were whittled out of whalebone by voyaging sailors with time on their hands. They were presented to their wives and sweethearts upon their return—a labor of love for a labor of love.

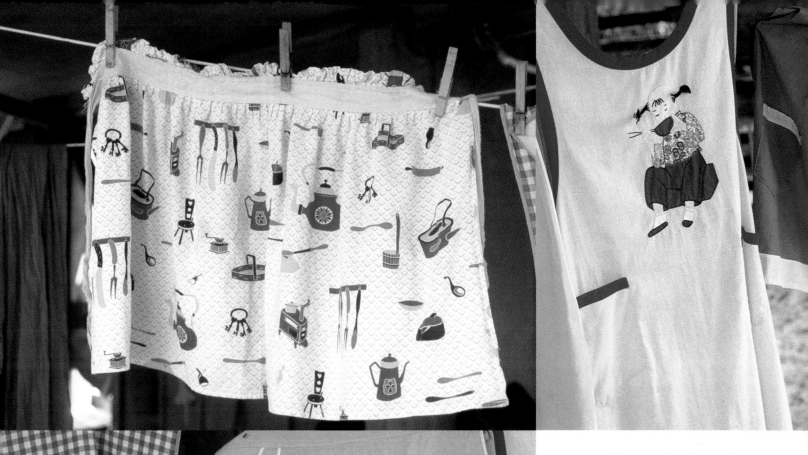

Above: Bib aprons like this one decorated with a hungry young pigtailed girl, are full-length aprons that tie at the waist with a bodice that extends above the waist and over the head. In the 1950s, probably the era of this handmade beauty, aprons were worn more as a fashion accessory than as a utility bib. I couldn't resist this one or its obvious mate, seen below, for $12, at Bermuda Triangle, Nags Head, North Carolina.

Top left: On the job, three spring-clip clothespins hold a skirt or half apron made of a cotton fabric displaying the kitchen tools of the trade. Plucked from a lively collection found at The Twila Zone, Nags Head, North Carolina, it was $5.

Bottom left: Two apron catches, made on the Outer Banks of North Carolina, hang side by side in this impromptu clothesline exhibition. The one on the left with a green-and-white-checked bib, another prize for $6 from The Twila Zone. The pink mate to the one seen above, this one is appliquéd with an early mode of travel in the Orient and was $14 at Bermuda Triangle.

33

Above: A hand-drawn advertisement for aprons created by a serious aficionado of apron collecting and wearing, Lisa Durfee.

It was a spontaneous kitchen fashion show of aprons choreographed in the doorway of our carriage house in upstate New York. I couldn't resist modeling them—sometimes twice—with the perfect kitchen couture accessories—mismatched oven mitts, seen in #5 and #7. Sharing the limelight, #9, was a hot model of the kitchen world, a hand-painted Mrs. Butterworth. Checks-on-checks was the statement made in #7. Of the undirty dozen presented here, prices ranged from 25 cents for #6 to $2 for #9. The strawberry pattern seen in #11 was only stamped on, and a spare piece of polka-dot fabric was safety-pinned to it. Lisa Durfee took it home from a street fair and did the embroidery and appliqués. I paid her $8 for it. Aprons #2 and #14 are barbecue aprons born in the 1950s for men to wear for backyard cooking events. Apron #12, actually a dish towel tucked into the waist of my jeans, allows a real aproned damsel to take a bow. It and the milk bottle (seen at table on page 13) are thanks to a generous loan from the Lisa Durfee kitchen and apron archives.

34

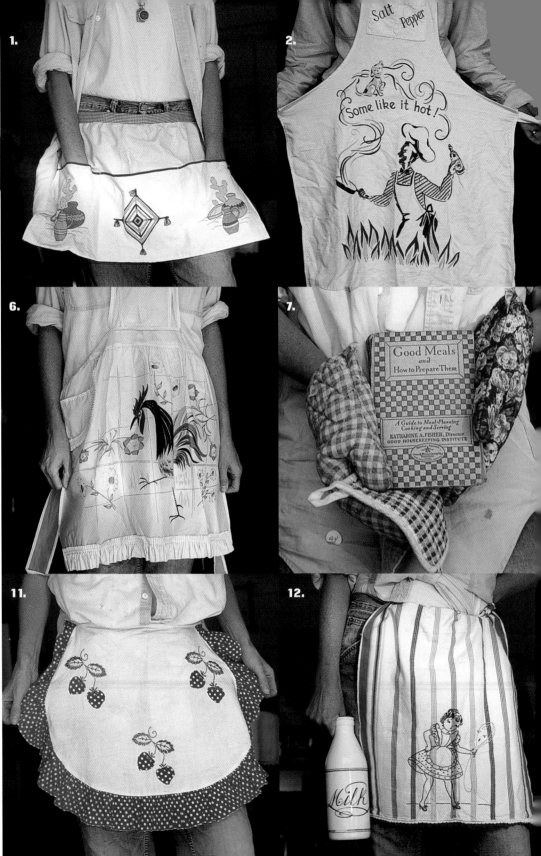

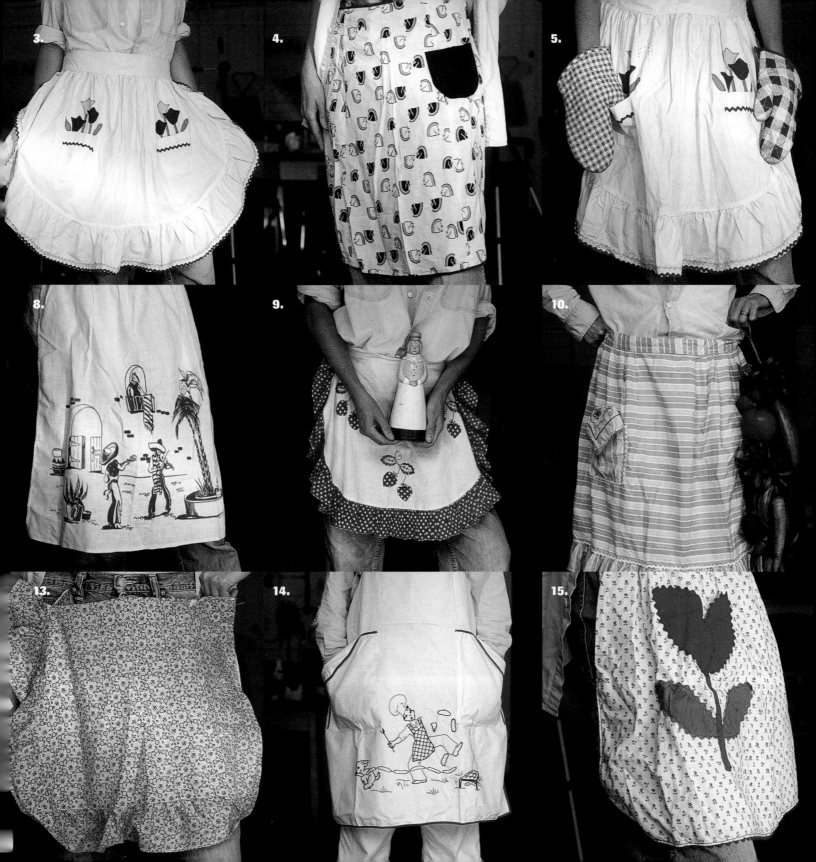

Clockwise from top left: 1. Best apron memory: going to my grandmother's house (we called her Ga-Ga) and tying a little apron onto a bottle of cold Coke. She had an array to choose from. The best part: a little pocket to stick the straw in. I hadn't thought of this childhood joy in decades, and then last summer there they were: five little bottle aprons for $1.25 from Merry-Go-Round Thrift Shop, Kill Devil Hills, North Carolina. **2.** From Lisa Durfee's aprons-on-dishtowels collection, this one she sprang $6 for. She couldn't resist the fine appliqué work (also in #5). "Can you believe," she asks, "they actually used these things after putting all that work into them?" **3.** A jovial chef outfitted in the equivalent of kitchen "scrubs"—an apron and chef's hat—is poised to operate with rolling pin in hand. More Lisa Durfee dish! **4.** An amazing remnant of those 1940s fabrics made in narrow (17-inch) width bolts specifically for kitchen curtains, place mats, towels, etc. Just cut and hem. The little dish towel motif reads, "Fun in the kitchen." Lisa Durfee dug up a a bunch of these scraps from Germantown Antiques Barn, Germantown, New York, for $4. **5.** Another of Lisa's appliquéd aproned kitchen towels. This busy homemaker's is polka-dotted. It was $4 from a forgotten antique shop. **6.** Lisa asks us to check out the bustier fit of the woman's apron and the man's stare! For $5, she calls it an "investment in sexist collectibles." **7.** A pair of aproned hostesses scurry across this 25-cent find (another Durfee special). The catch was that she had to embroider it herself following the prestamped pattern. It still had its original price tag attached: 29 cents. **8.** The Housewife's Crying Towel came in a $15 box lot, including the two barbecue aprons on the preceding pages. Lisa reports she had to work out a a lot of the stains (housewife's tears?) with Q-Tips dipped in diluted bleach.

THE DISH ON DISH TOWEL AND APRON CLEANUPS

According to Lisa Durfee, apron and dish towel queen (you can find her wares at the Germantown Antiques Barn, Germantown, New York, or check out her on-line auctions on www.ebay.com under durflink), there are no big secrets to cleaning up stained kitchen linens. Though she admits to clipping many an article on the subject and has heard passionate testimonials on everything from rhubarb roots to Electrasol Ultra, she still believes in good old-fashioned bleach and water. Sue Loomis, proprietor of Sue's Vintage Linens & Fabrics, St. Paul, Minnesota, agrees. Her tried-and-true method is to soak the aprons or towels in hot water in a mixture of equal parts Clorox 2 and dishwashing liquid. Soak as long as needed (these things are very colorfast) and rinse thoroughly. Hang to dry. If all else fails, Lisa's Plan B is to cut it up and turn it into something else. "If nothing else," she adds, "a stain is still a great bargaining chip during the haggling phase; no one has to know you might just get it out!"

a clean sweep

t was Mother Ann Lee, founder of the Shakers, who challenged her brethren to "Be neat and clean: for no unclean thing can enter heaven." If the message wasn't clear enough, she reiterated, "Clean your rooms well; for good spirits will not live where there is dirt. There is no dirt in heaven." These inducements to banish dust and dirt resulted in not only a clean living ethic but the tools to get the job done. Though the Shakers were not the originators of brooms and dustpans, they went a long way to promoting their use as well as to creating their own. It's the Native Americans we can thank for the first made-in-America brooms. Made of slender birch saplings with the ends splintered, they kicked off an industry of Dustbusters that swept the housewife off her feet by the Victorian era.

Preceding pages: A chorus line of dutiful duster-uppers, from decal to celluloid, for floor and table, a roundup deconstructed and described on pages 44-45.
Left: An exhibition of veteran brooms and brushes lined up Shaker-like in the utility corner of a make-believe kitchen (see more on pages 216-21) created in a carriage house stable in upstate New York.
Opposite: Close-up on clean. Top row, left to right: A wooden-handled veggie cleaner and twin scrub brushes—all from The Rummage Shoppe, Millerton, New York, for 50 cents each. Bottom row: A mini collection of mini-whisk brushes. The first on the far left, hung in a homemade string-fringed casing, $1 at Villa's Auction Gallery, Canaan, Connecticut; the pair of doll baby-size whiskers united on the far right were found far apart—the little red one from Fredie's Shack, Geneva, New York, the little brown one from Pat's Attic Treasures, White Stone, Virginia, both for $1. The whisk-worn pair in the center from American Junk, White Stone, Virginia, were a gift from my sister/partner Nell.

Above: My favorite dustpan measures 6 inches wide by 7^{1}/$_{2}$ inches long, to the end of the handle. Though it has the look of an early Shaker tin pan, I'm pretty sure it's machine-made of a sturdy metal. It's painted a blue that is reminiscent of old European enamelware. A little opening in the back of the handle allows me to hang it like a piece of sculpture, which is in my heart the way I see it. I think Claes Oldenburg would see it that way too. I paid $18 for it at Germantown Antiques Barn, Germantown, New York. I use it rarely, but when I do, it is to scoop up dainty dust and crumbs. Though I don't know its history, I believe it has carried many a load–the little dustpan that could–and needs a rest.

Right: My blue feather duster hanging not far from the blue dustpan, above, hasn't done one day's work! Shame on you, blue feather duster! In truth the fault is mine. I love the plastic Red Rooster wrapper so much that I can't put it to work. It was made in China, and I picked it up at one of those dollar stores for, yes, $1!

Opposite: You're weaving though grassy aisles of clutter on a hot day in July. A flash of yellow glinting from a galvanized bucket interrupts your stupor. It's "All" or nothing. A have-to-have that you know will be welcomed home for its usefulness. Something to wash the floors with or the car or the windows or the dog (the small one, not the large one!) . . . Yippee! Victory at the flea! This one was found at the Copake Auction, Copake, New York, for $2.50.

Clockwise from above: 1. A standard dustpan with a ribbed-bottom tray, decorated with flowered decals and pink paint–$1 from The Rummage Shoppe, Millerton, New York. **2.** The Fuller Brush Company sold not only brushes but also the perfect complement, the Fuller dustpan. This vertical scooper, with thumb handle and a hole (right above the famous name) to thread a string hanger through, was $5 at Northeast Antiques, Millerton, New York. **3.** Sleepy, on his own (away from the other six), sings out a favorite dwarf solo, "Whistle While You Work," on a tiny house-keeper's musical push sweeper. A bargain Fisher-Price toy for only $1 at the SoHo Flea Market, New York City. The handle's missing, so is a little paint, but other than that . . . **4.** Embedded in the top center of this 27-inch memory urn (a terra-cotta pipe transformed into a 3-D scrapbook with a layer of puttylike substance) is a gem-size dustpan, the souvenir of somebody else's childhood, and an impulsive bid (mine!) of $115, at Copake Auction, Copake, New York. **5.** Bissell's Little Queen stands just 32 inches tall, but it works like the real thing. Rummaged at The Rummage Shoppe, for $6.

44

Clockwise from left: 1. On a porch not far from Charleston, South Carolina, sit a trio of brooms and a utility dustpan with a long wooden handle to prevent back strain. **2.** An odd couple of dustpans: a shovellike Everlast painted red, $5 from The Watnot Shop, Hudson, New York, and a fine-featured, diminutive Deco-decorated crumb pan, $18 from & etc., South Pasadena, California. **3.** After the dust has been cleaned, Sam Hamilton (more on Sam on pages 204-5) stores it in her nifty red reproduction of those push trash cans designed in the 1940s for institutional use. **4.** A Sanitary Dust Pan with a Good Housekeeping seal of approval stamped right on it. The sanitation aspect is fulfilled by the door that automatically closes after the dust has been swept into the tray. The long wire handle triggers the door and saves the back. From Elephant's Trunk Bazaar, New Milford, Connecticut, for $12. **5.** At Bountiful, Venice, California, two workhorse dustpans decked out in festive colors. Who says holiday gifts have to be frivolous?

In *American Family Style*, written in 1988, there was the tale of a doormat that stood at the entrance of several of my family's doorways. The message, muddied by many family feet, read: "A perfectly kept house is the sign of a misspent life." How far is that from Mother Ann's Shaker philosophy? Far, but not so far. We all would love to live the clean, simple life of the Shakers, but for many of us a balance of some sort is what we seek. Each one of the nine children in my family had his or her chores, but along with the lessons of individual responsibility we learned another lesson: There is more to home than housework. Making a home warm and comfortable, making friends feel as welcome as family, were just as important as having everything in its place. One way to make friends feel like family, we learned, was putting them to work, helping us set the table, wash the dishes . . . sweep the floor!

Right: Domestic icons, all lined up, ready to serve their homeland, the kitchen. One that might not pass inspection—a once-proud stand-up dustpan (cousin to #4 on the previous page) a little worse for wear but ready for duty. Drafted into service from a neighbor's garage sale for $3. A Cosco utility step stool, circa 1950, props up the orders of the day in a book calendar from fifteen years earlier. Beneath it lies the foundation for all housewives of the day: *The Better Homes & Gardens Cook Book*, a revised edition from 1962, picked up for $12 at The Twila Zone, Nags Head, North Carolina. The charming pair of red-and-white-checked wedgies, the inspiration for the color coordination in this kitchen, was the highlight of a recent visit to Madalin, Tivoli, New York, for $8.

When Alice Reid bought her house in the Hudson Valley of New York, she got the old house she and her husband, Don, had always yearned for, a little stone dependency (more about that on page 62), a roomy barn to store and sell antiques, a large field for her large brood of Newfoundlands and Labradors to roam, and last, but not least, the old red metal dustpan guarding the back door of her home sweet home.

sinking spells

Susan Sarandon in the opening scene of *Atlantic City*, scantily clad, leaning over an old porcelain sink while sensuously scrubbing the smell of seafood off her hands and arms with freshly cut lemons, irrevocably changed the image of the kitchen's main command post. If it's true, as studies claim, that up to 50 percent of our time in the kitchen is spent planted at the sink, then thank you, Susan! Though dishwashers and washing machines have largely replaced the critical chores of the sink, it still remains the loading zone for the dishwasher, the central shower for fruits and vegetables, the well for cooking and cleaning, and in many ways the real energy source of the heart of our homes. New sinks are dressed up in stainless steel, enameled cast iron or steel, vitreous china, brass, and copper, but it's old white porcelain, galvanized steel, and rusty zinc that star in the vintage kitchen dramas about to unfold in a bungalow by the sea, an early Virginia farmhouse, a 1950s jewel, and an ancient hayloft with no running water. Kitchen theater junkers won't soon forget.

Left: Not Susan's lemons but grated lemons used for a lemon glaze on pound cake made by a friend's mother. More on Hortensia's cake, and the lineup of glasses on the following pages. **Preceding pages:** Close-up of a turn-of-the-century kitchen by the sea washed by the blue-and-white collection of a fair-haired prince of junk who has lovingly installed it piece by piece.

On a barrier island off Long Island's eastern shore, camouflaged by tall pines, stands (on tiptoes, it seems) a two-story red-roofed frame farmhouse built in 1875. But according to Mark Campbell, one of its owners, it was actually constructed on the other side of the Great South Bay and was either floated over or possibly driven across during one of those legendary winters when the bay froze to a concretelike ice. Whatever journey it made, its little red roof just barely sticking out above the treetops has been a landmark on the island since 1906. The wainscoted kitchen, seen at right and on pages 48 and 49, was added in the 1920s. It is entered through gardens Mark has painstakingly created over the last eight years by layering sand with hundreds of bags of soil shipped over by ferry, the only access to this island paradise. It is by far the most welcoming room of the house, as it is warmed with streams of sunlight and the smells of freshly baked pound cake (or something on that order) almost always emanating from the large friendly oven. My first impression as I stood in that fragrant doorway was that the sea had swirled through, leaving a mermaid's trousseau of blue-and-white china scattered in artful symmetry against the white wainscoted back wall that climbs up to the beamed roofline ceiling. In fact, it is the flotsam and jetsam of many flea market excursions navigated by Mark and longtime friends of this seaside pavilion of found objects and found dreams.

Above: An enamel soap dish punctuates the blue-and-white landscape with a spunky spot of green. It was found at the Twenty-sixth Street Flea Market, New York City, for $3.

Left: Five years ago a fastidious member of the household voted to add a dishwasher. Mark admits most of the time dishes are washed in the sink and air-dried on the old porcelain drainboard. (If something is missing, it's usually found in the dishwasher. "We tend to forget it's there," confesses Mark.) The four French agateware bowls, having just served up Hortensia's pound cake topped with a warm lemon glaze, take a time-out after a sink cleanup. Speckled in red, yellow, cobalt blue, and green, the four, along with the red-and-white-speckled spoon, were French finds at the Twenty-sixth Street Flea Market, each $10. The lineup of glasses, seen closeup on the preceding pages, are from the left: two new Itala glasses from Takashimaya, New York City, $10 each, and a pair of vintage cut glasses, two of many foraged from every yard sale possible on an average of 50 cents apiece. Endorsed by Mark as "the best for wine, champagne, or beer outside in the summer."

Opposite: In the kitchen's foreground, an old school desk scavenged from a yard sale in Patchogue, Long Island, for $5. It originally bore peeling old paint, but Mark refinished it as a more suitable eating-off table. The mismatched Windsor chairs were found on different Sundays for under $20 at the Twenty-sixth Street Flea Market. The home of the grated lemons seen on the opposite and preceding pages is the indispensable and glorious sculpted lemon pyramid holder, the centerpiece of the table (and the room!), another treasure from the Twenty-sixth Street Flea Market.

A summer house filled with lots of guests and, until five years ago, no dishwasher required some out-of-the-dish-drainer thinking. The solution? You're looking at it: Rubbermaid drainer shelves hung over the sink area so that washed dishes can go straight to their storage spaces and drip-dry. When the homeowners have a passion for plates, these racks become a double solution. Zoom in on the objects of desire. From left to right, the first five are Lu-Ray pastels collected for about $2 a plate; count ten plates in from far left and discover four ripple-edged mates, English stoneware that came with the house. Upon hearing that the garbage used to be buried on the island, Mark became a garbageologist and actually unearthed more stoneware in the backyard! Hence, plates, plates, and more plates.

Though some would argue the sanitary value of the dishwasher, think of all those great conversations had after a good meal, standing over the sink washing dishes with a friend. The constant dishwashing companion of my friend Bobby Ball (more on his kitchen seen on page 144) is the blackbird perched in his kitchen window. It was carved by a local Virginia artisan and was a gift from his friend Miriam Haynie, another artist/writer. Bobby's favorite dishes, draining to the right, are hand-painted southern pottery manufactured by Blue Ridge. He bought a whole set of them twenty years ago for "not much," he says, "maybe thirty dollars."

I never trust a kitchen without a dishdrainer. Mark Campbell's classic Rubbermaid, seen here in his summer kitchen, is always full. The original was introduced in 1947. It was the first wire dishdrainer coated in rubber latex to prevent the breakage and chipping of dishes. A vinyl coating was perfected later and is still on dishdraining duty today. The green plaid dishcloth and towel were from a boxed set from the 1940s, found at a flea market for a couple of bucks.

A friend of Stephen Drucker's once told him that Stephen had installed the kitchen everybody else wants to rip out. It has a gray linoleum floor, an old blender, an old mixer, an old toaster, and a period New York Central Railroad calendar. What he failed to list was the gleaming porcelain double sink (it's new) and the happy triple-stemmed cherry curtains brightening up the windows. They were plucked from the kitchen department of one of his favorite resources, Sage Street Antiques, Sag Harbor, New York, for $6.50. Stephen finds them "very optimistic." A siege of polka dots overtakes the nest of mixing bowls in the middle shelf of the cupboard. These bowls, a 1930s breed of custard glass, were found on opening day at Kitschen, New York City, almost ten years ago, for $20. The green tumblers below, manufactured by Anchor Hocking in the 1950s, were hunted down dot by dot for 50 cents apiece at random yard sales. The enameled steel lobster platter, below, was another Sage Street find for $8.50. The clear canister set to its right and the red set back up in the cupboard were each around $50. The red set was from Yard Sale, East Hampton, New York, and the clear ones from one of the many glass shows he haunts. The pristine dish cloths and towels stacked next to the sink collected for their labels at about $2.50 each at (yep!) Sage Street, are never used. The steel chair laced with red nylon from Anthropologie, New York City, was a gift. The streamlined silver drawer handles were searched out at Muff's, a used hardware store in Orange, California. How far will he go?

Return to the opening of this chapter, pages 48–49, and catch the cinemascope view of Mark Campbell's Technicolor kitchen production where romance rubs elbows with utility. The utility: a pair of very workable enamel colanders picked up at the Twenty-sixth Street Flea Market, New York City, for $8 and $12. The romance: a $5 metal monkey hanger, another find from the Twenty-sixth Street Flea Market, and a bronze Tibetan monastery bell that rings in the next meal from a local Greenwich Village shop (long gone) for around $25.

It was the kitchen of an eighty-six-year-old woman named Augustine that inspired this make-believe kitchen set in my barn in upstate New York. Augustine's kitchen in Hautes-Alpes, somewhere between Nice and Grenoble, not far from the Italian border, is perched high above a village clinging to the mountainside. I visited her through my friend Marie-France Boyer's amazing book *Really Rural* (Thames and Hudson, 1997). Her sink is actually an old porcelain sink with a ridged porcelain drain attached. Rust is something both share, but mine, seen above and at right, made of cast iron, has hers beat out by miles. Around Augustine's sink and throughout her kitchen are displayed not only the expected utilitarian objects of cooking and cleaning but greeting cards, stuffed toy animals, plastic dolls, plastic flowers, pieces of wrapping paper, and empty bottles. Her kitchen is a scrapbook—totally real, rural, and personal. With that kind of inspiration and my primitive red sink, I went about creating a kitchen set invested with the personal whimsy and rural spirit of Augustine's.

60

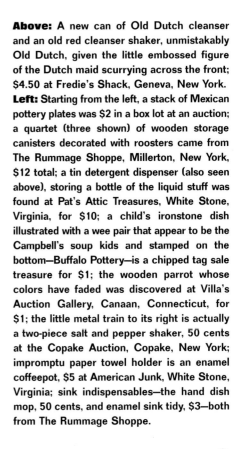

Above: A new can of Old Dutch cleanser and an old red cleanser shaker, unmistakably Old Dutch, given the little embossed figure of the Dutch maid scurrying across the front; $4.50 at Fredie's Shack, Geneva, New York.

Left: Starting from the left, a stack of Mexican pottery plates was $2 in a box lot at an auction; a quartet (three shown) of wooden storage canisters decorated with roosters came from The Rummage Shoppe, Millerton, New York, $12 total; a tin detergent dispenser (also seen above), storing a bottle of the liquid stuff was found at Pat's Attic Treasures, White Stone, Virginia, for $10; a child's ironstone dish illustrated with a wee pair that appear to be the Campbell's soup kids and stamped on the bottom—Buffalo Pottery—is a chipped tag sale treasure for $1; the wooden parrot whose colors have faded was discovered at Villa's Auction Gallery, Canaan, Connecticut, for $1; the little metal train to its right is actually a two-piece salt and pepper shaker, 50 cents at the Copake Auction, Copake, New York; impromptu paper towel holder is an enamel coffeepot, $5 at American Junk, White Stone, Virginia; sink indispensables—the hand dish mop, 50 cents, and enamel sink tidy, $3—both from The Rummage Shoppe.

Left: Alice Reid was cleaning out her barn! It was a hot July afternoon, and she was dreaming of moving to Maine. A collector by nature and an antique dealer by profession, she filled her barn with the overflow from her store and her nearby chock-full house. I was there in a flash. She had already dragged the huge utility sink outside, probably to clear the doorway. "Mine," was my greeting to her as I jumped out of the truck. "Yours!" was her greeting in return. The deal: $125. The history: a 48-inch long galvanized double utility sink, 13 inches deep, probably manufactured at the turn of the century. It was lodged in a little stone dependency outside Alice's main house, where the former owner did most of her cooking and canning. Her husband had worked at a nearby sanatorium and during a renovation in the 1930s rescued it from a trip to the dump.

Above: The average sink holds about five gallons of water. Why would you need one that holds at least five times that? Think of a potting shed basin, a roomy tub to wash your dog, a place to soak old quilts rescued from a flea market, a hundred plates and cups you just carried home from a box lot auction! I thought of all these things as I hauled my prized double sink into the back of the pickup. Sheltered temporarily against the back wall of our carriage house, it stores vagrant washboards (souvenirs of a past life) and another recent acquisition: a watermelon feast captured in oil. The painting, picked up at a tag sale for $5 at Villa's Antique Gallery in Canaan, Connecticut, inspires yet another deep sink task: icing those juicy, ripe fruits of summer just before the big seed-spitting contest! The armchair to its right, a comfy seat for a guitar strum, has endured an extended quarantine in the carriage house awaiting some upholstery work and an opening in the main house. Its embroidered back was the main attraction at the Copake Auction, Copake, New York, for $20.

Clockwise from top left: 1. Child's play from the 1950s, a kitchen sink, only 9 inches high, discovered with its mate, a matching miniature cupboard, in Fredie's Shack, Geneva, New York. The pair cost $45. Waiting a cleanup dip, a $10 set of toy metal kitchen implements with candy corn-colored handles of red and yellow plastic from & etc., South Pasadena, California. **2.** Sink tidies, first available in the 1900s, were triangular so they could lodge neatly in the corner of the old earthenware sinks. They were handy receptacles for scraps, coffee grains, and the like before the dishwashing began. This little orange one, a more contemporary version in plastic, has become the stage for a baby doll's fountain, hodgepodged together out of shells and stuff. Both were picked up at random tag sales for under $1. **3.** A miniature (3½-inch-high) green tin sink from the late 1920s to early 1930s is flanked by two Thumbalina-size wooden dolls, an aproned maid and chef, from Shoestring Antiques & Gallery, Norfolk, Connecticut, for $9. The sink was a sort-of-gift-with-purchase of the big galvanized one seen on the opposite page (see all three in their high-rise home on page 172). **4.** "How much is that kitchen in the window?," the one in Paula Rubenstein's New York City store? I was passing by on a SoHo stroll, and there was this perfect miniature model of a 1950s kitchen. When I discovered the price, I snapped a picture and was on my way.

stove heaven

It was my friend Stephen Drucker, gushing one day about his new (fifty years old) stove—a Wedgewood (with an extra *e*, not like the china) that turned me on to the ultimate resource for the born-again stove. Look not upward, but westward to South Central L.A., to 5415 South Western Avenue, to be exact, and you'll stand at the pearly gates (porcelain, more likely) of Antique Stove Heaven. According to the sign on the side of the building, it's WHERE THE GOOD ONES GO (see page 68). And after a complete restoration—rechroming, reporcelaining, custom coloring—it gets another go at a new kitchen life with a guardian angel like Stephen (who's on his second stove) or possibly, maybe, perhaps you!

Right: Stephen's Wedgewood in what he describes as his *Life* magazine 1948-style kitchen in East Hampton, New York. The stove cost about $800 and about $500 to get it to the East Coast—"about the same as a really good new stove and a lot less than a professional-quality stove. It has a broiler on the left, a stove on the right, a warming drawer, a chrome griddle, and four burners (two with flat cast-iron plates instead of the usual prongs). It's so finely tuned," boasts Stephen, "you can dial the burners back to a special simmer setting. And it has five pilots burning, which definitely help keep your kitchen warm during the winter." The mismatched kitchen tools over the stove he bought one at a time at yard sales and flea markets for 25 cents to $0.50, depending on the color (red is the most common) and how flaky the paint was.
Opposite: One of Stephen's favorite features of his Wedgewood (he sees it like a sleek Coupe de Ville) is the clock (it works) and the built-in salt and pepper shakers (new corks!). "You almost can't believe so much attention went into the design of an everyday appliance!" Stephen exclaims.
Preceding pages: A line up of pearly white born-again stoves at Antique Stove Heaven.

Clockwise from above: **1.** Stove Heaven's proclamation, WHERE THE GOOD ONES GO, for everyone to see on the side of its building in South Central Los Angeles. **2.** Election to the Stove Heaven's Hall of Fame! is largely influenced by its founder and the founder of the company, Winsor Williams. You'll see Wedgewoods, Western-Hollys, Danglers, Chambers, Jungers, Quick Meals, and Ropers from the early 1900s to the 1950s. **3.** A duo of Magic Chefs, circa 1920 to 1930s, are, according to Winsor Williams, the Ferraris of antique stoves. Restored models cost in the thousands. **4.** An avocado-toned O'Keefe & Merritt from the 1940s has a chrome griddle between the burners. **5.** Ranges from the 1940s and 1950s, like the O'Keefe & Merritts, came equipped with all the convenience gadgets but were also the most technologically advanced. Clock controls allowed the modern chef the option of putting the meal on automatic pilot. **6.** A tour through Antique Stove Heaven brings you face-to-face with artfully displayed walls of stove parts like errant cast-iron plates and burners. **7.** "How much is that yellow, pink, red stove in the window of Antique Stove Heaven?" Reds are by far the most popular and can typically cost several thousand dollars.

The homeless stove, seen at left, for sale at Holland's Stage Coach Markets, Gloucester, Virginia, could be a real steal, but consider the commitment. The one that comes to mind first is moving that hulk of metal. You could be talking about 600 pounds here. If that's the case, then bracing your kitchen floor may be the next commitment, particularly if yours is over somebody else's! In the summer 1997 issue of *Renovation Style* Andrea Caughey asks new buyers of old stoves to consider the factors of fuel, size, weight, insulation, finish, operating condition, and, most important, safety. Do you want to fuel your cooker with gas or electricity? Either is available, but consult your utility company to see which is more cost-efficient. An uninsulated stove can get red hot. Old insulation can be filled with grease and grime or even made of asbestos. Both are hazardous, so be very careful. Are all the parts intact? Is the porcelain chipped? Parts can be replaced, and cosmetic surgery performed, but be aware of hidden, escalating costs. Or forget this risky business and go directly to heaven, Antique Stove Heaven, that is, or a place like it. A true believer, Stephen Drucker swears on his cookbook that Stove Heaven actually "tests the thermostats and the burners, makes the stoves like new, has all the spare parts, and can diagnose any problem long distance." Or you can still plunk down 350 for the old thing at left and use it in your potting shed to cook up some great flower arrangements in those old rusty cookpots suspect for stew but perfect for nasturtiums. I did.

Clockwise from above: 1. Not far from Antique Stove Heaven, I braked for Twilight Zone Gift Thrift Store, where I spied the little compact cooker standing guard over all kinds of good stuff. I left the stove but picked up a great fishing vest for $3. Sometimes what lures you in is not the ultimate catch. **2.** An old porcelain Chambers stove spotted at Bowery Kitchen Supplies, Inc.; at the Chelsea Market, New York City. Though many of the old stoves have a couple of ovens, keep in mind most are smaller, and none is self-cleaning. **3.** Even I would have to say no! to this derelict stove. I'm not even sure it would work in the potting shed. Well, maybe. **4.** A Quality stove at Bowery Kitchen Supplies, Inc., priced at $1,200. **5.** A challenge, but not hopeless if you're an adventurer, at Holland's Stage Coach Markets, Gloucester, Virginia. **6.** Waiting for the garbage truck right outside my front door in New York City, an electric stove from the 1950s. **7.** A four-burner gas stove, circa 1950, abandoned on a city street by an apartment dweller perhaps inhibited by its minimalist style.

3.

4.

5.

7.

6.

HOME ON THE RANGE

Antique Stove Heaven's Winsor Williams recommends oven cleaner for the inside on everything except aluminum parts. "A glass cleaner or product, such as Formula 409 or Fantastik, can be used on the outside jacket of the stove, which is typically porcelain," he says. Use a small coat hanger to poke out grease in clogged burner holes. Surface grease can be removed by dousing the burners in a tub of household cleaner, such as Formula 409 or Fantastik, for a minute or two. Rinse and dry. Irregularities like chips, nicks, and cracks need to be repaired by a professional restorer.

matador's breakfast

It is the morning of the bullfight. The table is set for three—the matador and two aficionados. There is a portrait of the matador in the ring above the table. It is Pedro Romero, the nineteen-year-old matador from *The Sun Also Rises.*

> The boy stood very straight and unsmiling in his bull-fighting clothes. His jacket hung over the back of a chair. They were just finishing winding his sash. His black hair shone under the electric light. He wore a white linen shirt and the sword-handler finished his sash and stood up and stepped back. Pedro Romero nodded, seeming very far away and dignified when we shook hands.

It is July in Pamplona. The festival is about to begin with the running of the bulls through the streets to the ring. Romero will sit with his two friends before he departs for the bullfight. He will eat lightly and say very little. His thoughts are elsewhere. And his friends will understand that.

This is a fantasy, of course, inspired by Ernest Hemingway's masterpiece written in 1926. We are not in Pamplona. We are in my carriage house in upstate New York. The scene and the table have been set with real things foraged from flea markets and tag sales from California to New York. For just one chapter, let's pretend.

Above: The bullfight, my 30" x 50" oil, seen above and on the preceding pages, was the last thing I spotted at Rinaldi's Flea Market, Pleasant Valley, New York, on a hot Memorial Day weekend, a year ago. The masterpiece of my heart—$12—framed!

Opposite and preceding pages: The matador's breakfast is served on a unique handmade wooden folding table painted a blue close to the color of the bullfighter's pants. I found it folded up and ready to go at a moving sale only five miles from its present home. It moved me for $30. The curlicued wrought-iron garden chair is given a Spanish accent with the addition of the serapelike striped blanket, $10, at George Cole Auctioneers, Red Hook, New York.

Guess who's coming to breakfast? If you can believe the personalized cup below and in your face on the next page, then Papa is coming. And given the story we're writing here, then it has to be "Papa" Ernest Hemingway. The second guest, given the matador host, might be Lady Brett Ashley (heroine of *The Sun Also Rises*). The color of the table settings enriches a rather spartan repast of orange juice and nectarines.

Opposite, clockwise from top left: 1. Closeup of Papa's cup, a handmade gift for Daddy, finished with a green pearlized glaze and distinctive raised lettering. It was the one redeeming grace of an otherwise graceless estate sale in Falls Village, Connecticut. For 50 cents, it's a good prop in a fantasy breakfast, but not the vessel you would really want to sip your tea or coffee from, given the ragged terrain of its drinking rim. Beneath it lies a little ironstone plate decorated with a colorful Mexican couple decal, $1.50 from D's Place in Gloucester, Virginia. The silver plate spoon was one of a dozen picked up at a moving sale in Hillsdale, New York, for a quarter. **2.** Perfect nest for the nectarine centerpiece of this romantic breakfast drama: a delicate woven basket wound with a vine of tender leaves. Another treasure from D's Place, for $2. **3.** I found this little splotchy yellow pottery pitcher dribbled with green totally irresistible for $2 at Penny Paid, Locust Hill, Virginia. When its country of origin, Mexico, was revealed on the bottom, I knew in a second it would play a role in my Matador's Breakfast. **4.** My main obsesssion when traveling to Los Angeles is to make sure my visit overlaps a Sunday so I can get lost at one of the four mega outdoor flea markets that rotate from Veteran's Stadium in Long Beach (the third Sunday) to the Rose Bowl in Pasadena (the second Sunday) to the Pasadena City College campus in Pasadena (the first Sunday) to the south side of the Santa Monica Airport in Santa Monica (the fourth Sunday). The little white metal bowl and plate stenciled with abstract daisies—two pieces for $1—were a pair of three that I picked up on my last visit, which was on the third Sunday of the month, which would place that treasure's roots in Long Beach. **5.** My friend Alice Reid lent me her large glass rose pitcher and matching glasses to entertain my unseen guests. She insists it was meant for iced tea or lemonade but agrees it's a dandy idea for orange juice-starved patrons sick of those stingy little orange juice glasses. In the late 1910s, Alice suggests, you could have picked up the pitcher and six glasses for about $2.99. She bought it a few years ago, not at the five-and-dime unfortunately, for $25.

For travelers on the road to junk (for a matador's breakfast or otherwise) the journey is less about what is ultimately found and more about the stops, the people, and the experiences along the way. On Memorial Day weekend 1997 I followed a winding trail and many tag sale signs up a mountain in upstate New York to discover the Mexican pot seen at right and above. An elderly gentleman and his mother had, I discovered, made this tag sale an annual event. It was on the ground outside their trailer that I found several souvenir pots. They appeared to have spent the winter (maybe several) outdoors. They were covered in mud and networked with thin cracks, and I paid $1 for them, which in retrospect seemed to be the price of admission into the family's trailer, where they displayed their really special stuff. Each item came with a story told in such an earnest manner that I felt reluctant to uproot it from its history and home. The man and his mother were happy to see the pieces go with me. The journey is the destination.

Right: Both the orange cupboard, a homemade special discovered at Fredie's Shack, Geneva, New York, for $35, and the wooden soap powder pitcher, $12 at Madalin, Tivoli, New York, share the personal decorative touch of stickered decals. The portrait was rescued from a pile for $10, at a flea market not far from Great Barrington, Massachusetts.

82

The black wooden tray, displaying decals of a serenading
guitarist and his señorita, was
bought with the soap powder
dispenser, also with a decal
(opposite), at Madalin, Tivoli,
New York, for $16. Mexican
kitchen motifs such as these
were incredibly popular in the
late 1930s and early 1940s.
The painted metal zinnia, an
everlasting flower picked at
Penny Paid, Locust Hill,
Virginia, for $4, will bloom well
beyond breakfast. The fruitful
pair of salt and pepper shakers
flanking it, from Bermuda
Triangle, Nags Head, North
Carolina, echo the breakfast
menu. The wooden salad set
was 50 cents from Alpha &
Omega, Gloucester, Virginia.

Clockwise from top left: **1.** Made in Mexico, painted wooden trays—this one a slightly cracked tag sale bargain for 75 cents—are found everywhere. **2.** A set of four dried gourds starring a sombreroed hombre and dancing partner was likely painted up in Mexico or not far from the border. This set from Alice Reid's Antiques in the Barn, Livingston, New York, was $40. **3.** The frog prince in disguise! A school project that stole my heart at Rinaldi's Flea Market, Pleasant Valley, New York, for a prince of a price, $2. **4.** Along the lines of mosquito netting draped over a bed to protect the sleeper from annoying flying creatures, this wire cover protects the warm loaf beneath it. Covers like this of wire or muslin were made from the late 1870s until the 1950s. This one is enhanced with colorful raffia flowers and was probably from the latter era. I bought two for $24, at Northeast Antiques, Millerton, New York. **5.** A portrait of a lady (Lady Brett Ashley?), rescued from Copake Auction, Copake, New York, for $5. **6.** A gift for Lady Brett, or has she left it behind as a thank-you to her heroic host, or could it be for Papa H.? (You decide.) The delicate daffodil locket is not from Tiffany's but from the foragers' Tiffany's, The Rummage Shoppe, Millerton, New York, for $6. **7.** The matador's Barbie, a noseless replica, was bought so long ago I remember nothing, except the price, $5. **8.** The matador's brother in pink, in a precarious position. Matador and bull, both from Madalin, Tivoli, New York, for $15 each. **9.** A captain's chair from circa 1925 but painted and stenciled much later in the 1950s. This kind of chair was known in firehouses as the fireman's rocker because the firefighter would rock back and forth in it, waiting for the alarm to sound. One of three from Alice Reid's, $10 each. **10.** A wooden facsimile of a teapot—a handy storage bin and soap powder dispenser popular in the 1940s, seen previously on page 82, $22, from Madalin, Tivoli, New York. **11.** Cornucopia (sort of) salt and pepper shakers, seen on the previous page, $8, from Bermuda Triangle, Nags Head, North Carolina. **12.** An English cookie tin with a Spanish beat. It danced right off a flea market table for $1.

kitchen gallery

If the three bears moved to L.A., this is the bungalow they would inhabit. Unfortunately for them, it's been lived in for about ten years by a much less furry Poppa-Man, Eddie, Momma-Woman, Laurie, and Little Baby-Girl, Samantha Warner-Garrick. If you read *American Junk*, you met them way back in 1994, before Sam was born. Their story continues with a little less space but with just as much imagination. Their wild choices and mixes of colors seen on these pages were, according to Momma-Laurie, a way of imbuing this very basic, "boring 1950s ranch house with some (make that lots of) magic."

Preceding pages: Temporarily borrowed from the kitchen and displayed against the exterior avocado green wall off the back of the house are two kitchen art gotchas. Meaning when Laurie saw them it was an instant "gotcha, can't let you go" thing. On the left side is a glued-together arrangement of fruit resting in a very unusual double-based carved bowl, $100 from a now defunct folk-artsy gallery. At right is an antique Victorian wire basket loaded with glass-beaded (not the Styrofoam kind manufactured now) fruit, a gift from her mother, Corrine.

Opposite: "I wouldn't wear it to dinner at Spago," says Laurie, when asked about her favorite turquoise gaucho hat. But she would and does wear it to flea markets and museums, book fairs, and things like that. It has a fuchsia interior (more wild color!) and two faded roses blooming on the rim. She bought it from the same gallery mentioned above for $40.

Left: Laurie broke her $20 ceiling when she paid $65 for this painting, which is temporarily propped on the handcrafted chair by Adirondack artist Barry Gregson. She actually bought it for her mother at the Twenty-sixth Street Flea Market in New York City and later took it back from her! It's understandable, when you look at how closely it resembles the 1930s Mexican blanket, a satillo, she collected about five years ago for about $100 and the wooden sculpture of fruits and vegetables collected for $8 at the Long Beach Outdoor Market, Long Beach, California.

The pull-out-all-the-stops table setting, seen on the opposite page, is a testament to Laurie Warner's passion for exotic color and rich textural layerings. Without a doubt the mystery dinner guest who inspired this creation had to be none other than the romantic and passionate Mexican artist Frida Kahlo. Kahlo's own house in Coyoacán, Mexico City, now the Museo Frida Kahlo, embodies the same eclectic spirit as Laurie's and reveals Kahlo's insatiable passion for collecting objects, especially Mexican crafts. It is easy to imagine the artist pulling up the long skirts of her Tehuana dress as she settles into her chair and surveys with her glittering dark eyes the still life of color, shape, and texture spread out on the table before her. As she lifts her goblet, she is amazed at its lightness. It is in fact made from a gourd secured on a wooden base and painted. Our host, Laurie, discovered it at one of her favorite haunts in South Pasadena, David Yarborough on Mission Street, for $7.50. The compote of wooden fruit was a Laurie find for $5, at the Rose Bowl Flea Market, Pasadena, California.

Right top: Accessible storage for dish towels and napkins: a handcrafted basket (see it again on top of the fridge on page 94) topped with a strawberry painting picked up in a flea market in Newfane, Vermont, for $5.

Right middle: The napkins are a makeshift pair. The colorful plaid on the bottom is actually a dish towel; the smaller printed one is made of fabric from Indigo Seas, Santa Monica, California. The silver spoons, collected at various times from Gloria List, whose gallery is now in Santa Fe, are Navajo and cost from $30 to $100. Laurie mixes them with her real silver.

Right bottom: More wooden fruit, this time served up on a yellow wooden platter. Laurie's collection now totals about thirty. "Never enough," she sighs.

Above: The south-of-the-border dish towel and its mate, seen at right, were made from old 1950s curtain fabric, a gift from Laurie's mom.

One of the first things you'll spot along the south wall of the Warner-Garrick 9' x 15' kitchen is their forty-year-old O'Keefe & Merritt stove. It's lived there thirty years longer than they have—"one of the best features of the house," says Laurie. "It's a real workhorse stove. It just recently broke down for the first time ever. The repairman couldn't believe it had never been serviced!" (For more on vintage stoves, revisit page 64 and Antique Stove Heaven, Los Angeles, a great resource for vintage stoves—WHERE THE GOOD ONES GO.)

Right: Laurie's O'Keefe & Merritt, from the 1950s, when stoves were stoves. The blue rooster teapot was a store-bought Michael Graves edition (you can get a $35 cousin also designed by Graves at Target). To its left is a Guatemalan hanging basket for sleeping babies. Reports Laurie, it is to keep scorpions and other pests away. It was a baby gift from the friend who introduced us, photographer Pam Barkentin. "We use it to store sleeping fruit," Laurie informs.

The giant asparagus dominating the 10' x 10' wall to the right of the stove was created by Laurie and was the first piece to hang in her kitchen gallery. "It was simply a matter of trying to make something out of nothing. Just the way we painted the exterior walls all those crazy colors, we covered the inside walls with lots of crazy stuff. The asparagus started the fruits and veggies theme in the kitchen." That was five years ago. The only thing slowing them down is they've run out of space.

A guide to the exhibition, clockwise from top right: 1. A watermelon wedge painted by a fairly renowned Mexican artist, a gift from gallery owner Gloria List. **2.** Still life of fruit from a flea market in Manchester, Vermont, $15. **3.** Framed postcards of giant fruit, $40, from a store in Hoosick Falls, New York, the home of artist Grandma Moses. **4.** Life is a bowl or basket, in this case, of cherries. A Laurie-kind-of-kitchen still life discovered at the Rose Bowl Flea Market, Pasadena, California, for $8. **5.** Seed packet art, specifically beets, brought home from a flea market in Dorset, Vermont, for $1. **6.** Lemons carved in wood, for $5 from the Santa Monica Outdoor Market. It's backed with old bits of newspaper and a beer can flip tab to secure it to the wall. **7.** Laurie's Heart's Delite, a Florida citrus fruit sticker she picked up with the beets seed packet (#5) for another $1 and mounted on wood. **8.** A strawberry basket, a gift from Laurie's mother, who purchased it at Carriage Trade Antiques Center, Manchester Center, Vermont. "It's really too valuable to be up there, but . . ." **9.** A little piece of glass fruit given to Laurie as a child by her grand mother. **10.** A postcard announcement of a Haitian art show. Laurie made the pineapple frame. **11.** Another postcard of oversize fruit from Hoosick Falls. **12.** A miniature bowl of fruit drawn by Laurie's sister Cammie.

A gallery in a gallery—the refrigerator is the perfect domain for four-year-old Samantha to display her artistic bent proudly. The black-and-white magnets are compliments of another artist, her aunt Cammie, Laurie's sister. (More about fridge magnets on page 190.) The painted Popsicle stick bowl on top, left of the big basket of napkins seen previously on page 91, was brought back from Dorset, Vermont, found at a flea market there for $1.50. Towering above the art-camouflaged refrigerator is a slightly cubist painting on artist board. All great finds have stories behind them. Laurie's masterpiece is no exception. She was riveted to it at the Pasadena City College Flea Market (that's different from the Rose Bowl Flea Market, also in Pasadena but on the first Sunday of the month) and was not surprised, just chagrined, when the owner asked for $85. After much bickering back and forth and Laurie's moaning about going over her budget, the dealer finally asked her point-blank what her budget was. "I was embarrassed to admit it was twenty dollars, but somehow I blurted it out." "Twenty dollars it is," said the dealer. "After all that, I really felt ashamed to take it for so little, but obviously I did," confesses Laurie. She points out the compote of fruit in the left side of the painting. "That qualified it for the kitchen gallery."

Right: You can make your fridge a piece of art (just as Samantha has) by attaching homemade masterpieces to it with magnets or masking tape.

The clock in our kitchen in New York City has hung over the door for about twenty-three years. (See page 195 for more on collecting clocks and the full story on ours.) I would love a penny for every time I have glanced up at it in the morning while reaching for a second cup of coffee and wondering if I really have time to enjoy it. At night I marvel at how late it is to be having dinner. The obvious point is that the clock is not just the timepiece but the centerpiece of the kitchen. Over the years there have been hours or maybe a day when the clock stopped or was broken. The kitchen became a black hole, a timeless void that gave no permission to have a second cup of coffee or to feel sorry for having dinner so late. That's why we were never without it for long. It was the kitchen conscience. All this personal history is to ensure your understanding of the shock I felt when Laurie related to me the history of her kitchen clock, which was recently purchased at the Los Angeles County Museum. It is a reproduction of a design by art nouveau architect and designer Charles Rennie Mackintosh. It was not that it was a new clock, a designer clock, a black-and-white clock that took me back. It was the revelation that this was in fact their first kitchen clock. Laurie admitted to a very long and tempestuous struggle to find the right timekeeper. But there must have been a hidden clock somewhere? She says no. Built into the top of the O'Keefe & Merritt perhaps? Again no. The pumpkin tin below the Mackintosh clock was harvested from The Shaker Museum, Chatham, New York, for $10.

Above: View of the kitchen exhibition through the backyard window. The leaded glass window, one of two, replaced a pair of "really horrible" predecessors and were salvaged for $40 each at a flea market.

I think I would have really liked E. M. Forster. He knew how a room with a view could totally affect not only the look of a room but its feeling and ultimately the feelings of the person staying or living in it. Though Laurie Warner and Eddie Garrick were able to replace the "really horrible" windows that had framed their view, there was little they could do with the view itself. A cinder-block wall does not offer too many creative solutions. Theirs: Camouflage it with as many growing things as possible and with as much shocking color.

Right: Inside looking out, the opposite view from the one seen above highlights the Technicolor color of the cinder-block retaining wall, the only revenge for such a view. On the center of the ledge, the angel of the kitchen, a Michael Graves bottle opener. The diminutive pottery vase to its left holds a tiny pinecone souvenir from a walk with Samantha. The scrub brush tied up like just-reaped wheat is a Shaker scrub brush. The musk ox, carved by the Eskimos in soapstone, was a souvenir to Samantha from Eddie. Protecting the right is a funny little devil monkey door knocker found at a Dorset, Vermont, flea market for a few bucks.

moveable feast

When the weather heats up, so does the kitchen. Hang out your Closed sign, and move the kitchen and the cooking outdoors. Haul out all that tacky plastic stuff you've been collecting at tag sales all winter, and have yourself a moveable feast (with apologies to Ernest Hemingway). If you haven't been squirreling away plastic through the off-season, don't feel disadvantaged. Plastic picnic trays and mugs, mustard and ketchup squeezers, corncob holders, thermoses, pitchers, and picnic baskets are the stuff yard sales are made of—all year long!

Left: The table is set with a stack of plastic picnic trays and mugs (at left), $1 each at a Memorial Day tag sale. The classic striped umbrella giant tumbler and its matching pitcher were $5 and $7, respectively, at Villa's Auction Gallery, Canaan, Connecticut. The classic metal plaid picnic basket was $5 at a neighborhood church bazaar. The ketchup, relish, and mustard jar set was $3 at a yard sale in Kilmarnock, Virginia. The four thermoses picked up at various thrift shops were on average $6. More about the mustard and ketchup squeeze bottles, cob holders, and the toothpick holder, to their left, on the following page. The stack of striped polystyrene bowls were 50 cents each at The Rummage Shoppe, Millerton, New York. The flowery metal salt and peppers were from the same yard sale in Kilmarnock where I picked up the condiment jars. The napkins, 25 cents, are part of an ongoing dig through bags at all kinds of sales.

Preceding pages: The "mover" behind my "moveable feast" is the pushcart picnic table I grabbed for $5 at Copake Auction, Copake, New York. The polka-dotted folding chairs, stored in their winter habitat on page 22, were discovered at an estate sale in Hillsdale, New York, four for $8. The large Scotch plaid metal picnic basket, stamped with a wee Scottish lassie, is far from an import. It was made in Burlington, New Jersey, by Chinco, Inc., and purchased for $10 at a very American tag sale in upstate New York. The red-and-white lunch pail perched on the chair to its right was picked out at The Watnot Shop, Hudson, New York, for $20.

Above: A way to rein in that hot buttered slippery piece of corn: Place it in its own little corn corral. This one from Nannie & Pop Pop's Attic, Shawboro, North Carolina, for $1.50.

Corn on the cob is to summer what apples are to fall. Everyone has a point of view on the best way to cook it and eat it. For some-like-it-hot corn right out of the pot or off the grill, corncob holders do the job (and have since the 1950s plastic boom). Lisa Durfee (whom you met on page 34) has two sets: a trio of yellow and green ones, seen in front of the jar, and a solid yellow set spread out in front of the jar and stored inside. The trio cost a quarter; the solid yellows, "fifty cents at most," she recalls. They are stored in the little jar because "I love the blue cap," she says but confesses to never using them for corn consumption. They're utility kitchen art. Lisa acknowledges that though plastic corncob holders have been around for decades, hers are probably not so old. "And the new ones," she suggests, "aren't that different from their tag sale sisters—except, of course, the price!"

Left: The "Sqeeze-Pleeze for Mustard" bottle and its squeezable ketchup mate were $3 from L & C Owens Antiques, White Stone, Virginia. It goes without saying where there's corn on the cob, there're toothpicks. A handy way to bring them respectably to the table is in this little toothpick dispenser, a West Coast find at Cookin', San Francisco, for $8.

As much as I do love a summer slice of watermelon, given the choice of eating it or displaying it as a summer centerpiece, I'd (surprised?) choose the latter. Ellen O'Neill has solved the problem with a papier-mâché version (see page 128) that she revels in all year long. I do have a large wooden slice carved by American folk artist Miles Carpenter, displayed for many years among shelves of stuff in our apartment in New York City (if you have my first book, *American Family Style*, you can revisit it on page 102). But other than the watermelon eaters painting (see page 62) up in the country, I have none. That was until last winter. Browsing through the jumbled tables of stuff set up in a parking lot on Broadway at Grand Street, known on Saturdays and Sundays as the SoHo Flea Market, I came upon the closest thing yet to my forever watermelon: six watermelon slice plates. On that frigid day not too many people were dreaming of watermelons (with possibly one exception), which probably accounts for the good deal I got: $5 for all six.

Right: My set of six watermelon plates, made in Italy, are ready to serve up a redundant slice the following summer. The red-and-white-checked napkins (for more checkered lives, see pages 16–17) were assembled napkin by napkin by patiently digging through bags and stacks of vintage textiles. Average price: 10 cents to a quarter each.

Above: A green metal faux wicker picnic basket with real wooden handles, costs $8 at The Watnot Shop, Hudson, New York. My collection of picnic baskets surpassed the limit for normal family picnic quotient years ago. I think I have at least two dozen in different sizes, constructions, and materials. I love the way they look all stacked together on a high shelf in my carriage house (see *American Junk*, page 92). Occasionally I recruit them for nonpicnic responsibilities, such as storing small collectibles, dish towels, or vintage flatware. Liven up the top of a desk by putting them to work as portable file cabinets.

Right: A picnic chorus line of ceramic-handled butter knives. From left to right, lettuce, carrot, pickle (or cucumber?), pepper, corn, and peas in the pod. Measuring only 4¹/₂ inches long, they're dandy not only for spreading butter but for cheeses and dips and for setting a doll's banquet table. I unearthed them in the layers of stuff at D's Place at Holland's Stage Coach Markets, Gloucester, Virginia, for $1 apiece.

Opposite, clockwise from top left:
1. Some dealers specialize in kitchen collectibles. This one set up at the SoHo Flea Market in New York City, insists on setting out her wares in a very colorful way. Picnic pick: the thermos, a cousin to those seen on page 101. Its red plastic screw top/drinking cup designates it as a 1950s model. Cost: $12. **2.** The fun side of plastics can be their surprising colors. Cases in point: the orange drainer, 50 cents, and the green plastic top on the syrup pourer, $1.79, both from L & C Owens Antiques, White Stone, Virginia. **3.** The "Squeeze-Pleeze" mustard dispenser and ketchup mate conjure up a backyard cookout in the 1950s. You can smell the hot dogs and burgers overseen by a weekend chef not unlike the one illustrated on the dispensers. $3 at L & C Owens. **4.** A variation of the picnic theme: the patio snack set, a plate that serves as a tray with an indent for the cups. I bought it for the packaging alone, $8, at The Carriage Factory Antique Center, Flint, New York. **6.** A napkin ring menagerie dating from 1935 to 1942. Bunnies, robins, fish, elephants, and scotties made of a plastic called Catalin. These from Once Upon a Table, Pittsfield, Massachusetts, range in price from $45 to $65. (Junk they are not!) **7.** What stood out on this shelf of thrift shop glassware was what I refer to as the orange juice striped glass pitcher. I added it to my collection for $6. **8.** A box of kitchen utensils priced at $1 each. (See how you might transform a plastic spatula into kitchen art on pages 198-99.) Don't let a sign at a flea market deter you from seeking a better price. Pick up three of your favorites, put on your friendliest smile, and try, "How about three for a dollar?" Maybe you'll get two!

109

chicken coop

W

hy did the chicken cross the road? To get to the little chicken coop across from our farmhouse in upstate New York. Our neighbor Elsie Albig remembers it when she was a child in the early 1930s. About two dozen Rhode Island Reds inhabited the cozy 9' x 12' space. They kept the family across the street well supplied with fresh brown eggs and occasionally a roaster on the table. After the chickens departed, garden tools moved in, and for a few summers, the owner's sister. Two summers ago chickens and roosters reclaimed their roost. If you tiptoe to the door, you won't hear their scratching and clucking, and you unfortunately won't gather any eggs. This chicken coop is more like a country branch of Madame Tussaud's. The chickens are made of wood, plaster, tin, plastic, paint, cotton, straw, paper, pottery, and papier-mâché. It's a cock-a-doodle-doo collection for posterity.

Preceding pages: On the left, the coop's open door welcomes two of the feathery residents, seen close up at right. The wooden stand-ins were picked up at an auction by Nell Thompson, my sister and junk partner, at American Junk, our junk outlet in White Stone, Virginia. The galvanized feeder was provided by Alice Reid of Alice Reid's Antiques in the Barn, Livingston, New York, for $35.

In this coop anything that goes with green goes! It was the interior paint color chosen long ago, so with the exception of the inhabitants, it rules the roost. Casting your eye around, catch the green farm table (opposite) tacked with green oilcloth, $5, from Copake Auction, Copake, New York; the green chair to its left, one of a pair—$1 apiece, also at Copake. The feed bag rug laid at the entrance to clean muddy claws was $1 from a lot at George Cole Auctioneers, Red Hook, New York. At left is the green starburst stovepipe cover, $3 at a barn sale in Pine Plains, New York; the green-and-white-checked napkin, 25 cents from a box lot at Copake Auction, is set beside the green-rimmed diner plates, $1 each from L & C Owens Antiques, White Stone, Virginia; the green-handled cookie cutters to their right (they used to be green!) and above were 25 cents each from The Rummage Shoppe, Millerton, New York; the matching mugs stacked on the table (opposite) were $2 at Thriftique, Millerton, New York. Not sporting green are the feathered pair on the table at left. The cocky plaster rooster was $4 at a Copake Auction tag sale, the prized glass hen nest (cousins seen earlier on pages 11–12 and more to come on page 117) was a $6 yard sale winner. The wooden beauty on the opposite page is a rare Canadian breed, transported by Mike Fallon to the Copake Auction annual Memorial Day sale—a $40 cock-a-doodle-doo.

It's Saturday morning, and I'm set for a day on the yard sale trail. My first stop is just a few miles away from Elm Glen Farm. It's advertised to open at 9:00 A.M., but I'm there at quarter of. The owners are still dragging their wares out of the garage. I spot four great metal yard chairs, and within two minutes, before another car drives up, they're loaded into the back of mine. The little green trolley at right is really an afterthought. The owner had jerry-rigged it with an extension cord for some garage shop projects. I bought it for $3. When the chicken coop green scheme came together, it fit right in as a storage tower for vintage egg cartons (four for $1), free berry boxes, and a couple of transient chicken coop tenants. The one on the left, a little painted tin windup toy from the 1940s that lays miniature eggs, cost $15 a decade ago. A brief bio on the straw hen follows on page 121.

Opposite, clockwise from top left: 1. An embroidered hen potholder, $2 from Madalin, Tivoli, New York; small painted wooden hen, $1, Thriftique, Millerton, New York; what looks like a paint-by-number chicken, $2 from Richmond Antiques & Flea Market, Richmond, Virginia; a pair of rooster shakers, $5, L & C Owens Antiques, White Stone, Virginia. Rooster-motif apron, $8, D's Place at Holland's Stage Coach Markets, Gloucester, Virginia. 2. To get you up in the morning, a rooster percolator, for $8 at Sharon Bramson's annual Memorial Day barn sale in Hillsdale, New York. 3. A painted-rooster tile, perfect for $5 until I knocked it to the floor. Scene of the accident and purchase: Fredie's Shack, Geneva, New York. 4. Ready to hatch the list of your choice, a handcrafted and painted clipboard with a message, "Don't sit on it!," $1.50, The Rummage Shoppe, Millerton, New York.

It was the evening of October 25, 1994. Driving into New York City, I tuned into National Public Radio's *All Things Considered*. The things considered that night by Bailey White, a first-grade teacher turned writer from South Georgia, were E. B. White and chickens. Ms. White was simultaneously mourning the recent passing of the great writer and at the same time extolling the virtues of chickens. Listening between the lines, one guessed that a lot of what she knew about chickens she learned from E. B. White. "A flock of hens will crouch down and face north when the evil eye is turned on them," she revealed, "and even hungry chickens will refuse to eat in the presence of a ghost." The spring after Mr. White's death she received a poultry and supply catalog, and under its influence (and we gather his), she ordered twenty-five New Hampshire Reds. The first night surveying them happily at home in their new digs, she hears a hinge squeak, and in walks E. B. White. "He was wearing baggy khaki pants with cuffs and a long-sleeve white shirt. He squatted down in the shavings beside me. His shoes were plain brown lace-up shoes. Without a word, he reached out to the nest of drowsy chickens, he opened his fingers, and in his hand was chicken feed." At first the chickens refuse the feed. But then one little chick steps forward and then another, and soon they are all pecking away at the feed in E. B. White's hand. "And I should have known it," she signs off. "For certain ghosts, chickens will make an exception."

Waiting for E. B. White, from left to right—a papier-mâché rooster, $20, from Tomorrow's Treasures, Pleasant Valley, New York; a miniature rooster, $1, facing its puffed-up friend, $8, nesting on two egg salt and pepper shakers, seen on page 121, are both from L & C Owens Antiques, White Stone Virginia; another nester (without eggs), $3, from Skrookie's 5 & 20 Antiques and Collectibles, Waterloo, New York; a pottery statuette, a cousin of the second pair, $5 from L & C Owens; a store-bought plastic hen that normally comes with baby chicks and legs, of course—a child's castoff found in my family's barn, where else? The oil painting framed on the wall behind them was retrieved from a church bazaar tag sale for under $20 more than eight years ago and until recently hung in our kitchen across the road.

Above: A loving-hands-at-home granny hen (glasses and all) nests in her own basket on the coop's stoop. Her ticket to ride? Just $2 from Thriftique, Millerton, New York.

The wake-up call was the rooster's burden long before the hotel operator's. Weather vanes were their territory, not only to forecast the wind's direction but to ward off evil. By the 1940s the rooster was off the roof and into the kitchen as the barnyard icon for everything from kitchen tableware to towels to tumblers. At least a dozen large manufacturers of tableware adopted the rooster as their pet pattern starting in the 1950s. The one at right, a found gift from my family's barn, was probably a wedding gift reject from one of my sisters. (I'll never say!)

Right: You can almost hear the wake-up call from the rooster on the platter and pitcher, manufactured in the mid-1950s. They hailed from a box stored in my family's barn in Virginia. The papier-mâché hen, made in Mexico, was $4 at a garage sale we visited en route from New York to Virginia. Be sure to protect yourself and those who take the unknown risk of driving behind you with a bumper sticker with a warning—I BRAKE FOR JUNK. (Look in the Junk Guide under Virginia, American Junk.)

Opposite, clockwise from top left: 1. Salt and pepper shakers nesting in a china base with a mother hen to cover when not in use. She and her large and small mates, plus the ironstone diner plates, a package deal for $20, from L & C Owens Antiques, White Stone, Virginia. **2.** A needlepoint feathered lady-in-waiting bides her time holding paper napkins—a $2 chicken delight from Nannie & Pop Pop's Attic, Shawboro, North Carolina. **3.** That ubiquitous rooster, stamped this time on the base of a handy hang-up cutting board, 50 cents from Merry-Go-Round Thrift Shop, Kill Devil Hills, North Carolina. **4.** A pair of royal rooster salt and pepper shakers, tag sale booty for $1, guard Her Highness the hen—a plaster hen nest top for a quarter at the Merry-Go-Round Thrift Shop. **5.** A pyramid of hen pitchers made in Japan, found at a tag sale for $4. **6.** Could that be Chicken Little, surrounded by giant plaster wall fruit, a daisy napkin holder, and a petite farm girl dwarfed by her giant sweet potato? Not unless chickens have changed their stripes! This miniature barnyard heaven produced by tag sale leftovers was scooped up in Irwin, Pennsylvania, for $5. **7.** Love on the farm depicted on a folksy tin tray retrieved from Kitty Hawk Thrift, Consignment & Antiques, Kitty Hawk, North Carolina, for $6. **8.** To wake up your coffee with a little cream and sugar, a pair of crowers, $7, Tomorrow's Treasures, Pleasant Valley, New York. **9.** Ruling the roost at Evarsky's annex of Tomorrow's Treasures, a slightly disabled papier-mâché rooster, $8. **10.** Charmed by the cover illustration, I snapped up this children's storybook at Fredie's Shack, Geneva, New York, for $3. **11.** A handmade rooster makes room for spools of thread and pins and needles on his pin cushion wing. Twenty dollars seemed exorbitant, but I had to have it at a Virginia flea market. **12.** Propped into a cozy little window at Bobby Ball's Virginia farmhouse is a metal temperature gauge selling country fresh eggs. It was a gift from friends. **13.** A trio of rooster stuff: a crowing cock pitcher, $2.50, a straw nester, $3, and electric coffeepot, $8, both seen previously on page 114 and gathered at Sharon Bramson's barn sale, 36 Hunt Road, Hillsdale, New York, held every Memorial Day, Fourth of July, and Labor Day weekend.

11 ellen street

It was five years ago, Memorial Day 1993, to be exact, that Ellen O'Neill walked through the gate, seen above, to her own sweet home in a little seafaring town off the coast of Long Island. Ellen (no stranger to you if you have followed her ongoing junk sagas chronicled in *American Junk*, 1994, and subsequently in *Garden Junk*, 1997) calls it "lucky eleven," recalling the luck, prayers, and statue of St. Joseph she buried in the backyard that tipped fate and the number 11 into her life. One big draw was the kitchen, seen at left. "Most people would have gutted it." Ellen laughs. "I haven't changed anything, except the floor and the sink. I love the old tongue-and-groove walls, the stove with the water heater tucked behind it, the funny black pipe." She catches her breath. "Everyone seems to gravitate to the kitchen," she continues, "probably because it's the largest and the sunniest room. There are six doors and three windows. It's where everyone collides and converges." (A friend once described it as "the perfect 1940s homemaker installation.") "My mother loves this kitchen; my brother wrote a book in it. It's definitely got an allure, but for me its just the place I feed the cat and make tea or coffee."

Above: The entrance gate to number 11 has probably been there just as long as the house, which was built in 1885. "It offers a wear and tear welcome and a nice click when it closes behind you," confides its owner with apparent pride.
Left: According to Ellen, the kitchen table is the perfect square proportion for the room. She hauled it home from a yard sale in Southampton, New York, for $125—"very expensive," she admits. The "strange little chair," a kind of cross between a chair and a stool, she found for $17 in Pennsylvania. The window valances are dishcloths–two on each window, a set of four for $10. "Blessed Mother blue" is how she describes the valances, the squares of the tablecloth, and those on the floor, which replaced "horrible faux red bricks."

The white stove, detailed in black, the utility design of the water heater behind it (she had to replace it a year ago and wouldn't have it moved—"that's where it belongs. It's a still life that shall ever be," she pronounces), the quirky black pipe that looms like a giant egret in silhouette behind the stove, the black-and-white chipped kettle and covered pot, seen at right, the white ironstone and porcelain pitcher on the white convent table—these are snapshots of Ellen O'Neill's perfect kitchen. It's part utility, part sanitary, antimachine, as-is, as-it-was, no frills, no cushions, Blessed Mother blue and white with accents of camp green. Ellen calls it a convent-clean kitchen in a Catholic hospital in the 1940s—welcome home!

Right: The kettle and its partner are intentionally placed on the back grills of the stove. It's a set composition that Ellen designed to complement the overall design of the stove and the water heater behind it. She chose the white enamel kettle, $8, from Sage Street Antiques, Sag Harbor, New York, for its sanitary appeal. She boils her water in the aluminum teakettle seen on top of the stove on page 122. This one is used exclusively to water her plants. The covered pot to its right was $1 at a yard sale. Her mother assures her, "There is a reason for that!" We extrapolate her meaning, eyeing the large chip apparent on the pot's top. One guesses there are more hidden inside. Health hazards are avoided since Ellen has no intention of boiling up more than a pot of bleach to whiten some vintage linens. (See page 139 for Ellen's recipe for laundering old linens.)

Not surprisingly, Ellen O'Neill actually likes to wash dishes. She would never own a dishwasher ("You must be kidding. I wouldn't want to sacrifice the view!"). The one modernization attempt made by the former owners failed, in her estimation. It was the installation of a "perfectly awful stainless steel sink!" Ellen replaced it with a "new" old one, a duplicate of the old-fashioned porcelain sink that she had loved in her last kitchen (seen in *American Junk*, page 98). She found it at The Brass Knob in Washington, D.C., for $175. She framed it in with tongue and groove to match the rest of the kitchen. The bracketed shelf above it supports a "conglomeration of things unused but needed just the same." Highlights from left to right: a ribbed green teapot; the For Rent sign, behind it, found in the basement; a green *O* for O'Neill or "Oh, no!"; a green cloth ledger from Anthropologie, New York City; and a tin cake keeper, "an old friend" she collected years ago for $12 in Pennsylvania. Art imitates life in a color photograph taken of the sink and hanging above it—a gift from her friend and photographer Henry Bourne.

Left: "My sink provides water for my cat, water for my plants, and water for my tea," lists Ellen. And then, of course, there's water for the dishes that are scrubbed with her favorite 100 percent cotton fiber dish mop ("with a nice green wooden handle") standing erect next to the sink. A 100 percent cotton dish towel is ready for duty on a "very useful" towel rack that is secured a short reach away. The Rubbermaid dish drain calls to mind others seen earlier on pages 56–57.

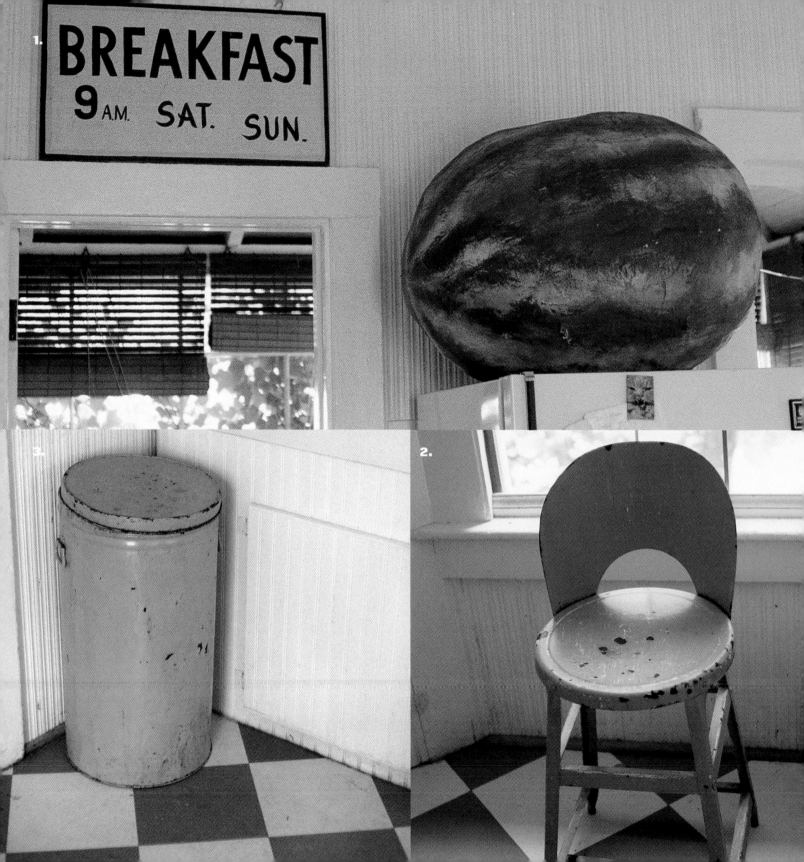

"Everything took on the blue-and-white checked thing," is the way Ellen O'Neill explains how the color palette for her kitchen evolved. But to her mind it is the camp green accents, mostly in metal, that took the blue-and-white thing off course and inevitably made the look less predictable, more Ellen. None of this was planned really. For instance, the green dustpan seen at left. Her mother, who sometimes questions her motives for purchases, questioned this one: "Why are you buying *that prize*?" Ellen's quick response: "It's my kind of art." Affordable too at a yard sale price of $2. Does she ever take it off its gallery hook to clean with? "Never! It's an art piece." Which essentially sums up her philosophy on the rest of her green collection exhibited on these pages.

Opposite: 1. No one who knows Ellen would fall for the breakfast days and hours listed on her breakfast sign precariously poised over one of the three kitchen windows. It's art, not reality. For $1 at a yard sale. The giant watermelon overwhelming the top of her refrigerator was once on display in the window of a prestigious designer store on Madison Avenue. She drooled over it to influential friends who worked there, and now her friends drool over it, thinking it's ripe from the garden. Foiled again. It's papier-mâché! **2.** The little green metal chair followed Ellen from her last kitchen, featured in *American Junk*, page 98. She picked it up for $18 at the Southampton antiques show. "It's not the kind of chair you get comfortable in," notes Ellen. "Utility is its attribute." **3.** The big green can she uses for garbage (see it next to the sink on page 126) is another according to Ellen, "mother irritant." "Can't we do better than this?" she implores on every visit. No conventional garbage bags fit it, but Ellen insists it's just perfect. It was toted back from an antique market in Pennsylvania for $6.

Above: Just outside the kitchen in the dining room is an original corner cupboard. It's the formal cupboard vs. the informal kitchen cupboard, seen at left. It contains mostly ironstone pieces—lots of pitchers and doll dishes. Ellen's review of what's inside: "Most have cracks; many are handleless; most do hold fluids and cost anywhere from one dollar to twenty dollars." Below it is a topsy-turvy pile of blue-and-white table linens. Folded, Ellen? "Tossed and never ironed. Why pretend?"

Left: Observable and accessible in the top stories of the kitchen's sturdy corner cupboard are what Ellen refers to as "blue-and-white orphan cups." The shades of blue from the fluted mixing bowl on the top shelf, far left, to the triple stack of cups exemplify the subtle shades of her designated Blessed Mother blue. *The Home Menu Cook Book* can be seen in a red-checked version back on page 19. Turn the page for a close-up on the one at the far left. The big green bread box up top used to be a place to stash money. Having exposed that hideaway, she will have to designate another use for it. Storing bread, perhaps? It was found at one of her favorite resources, Sage Street Antiques, Sag Harbor, New York, for $12.

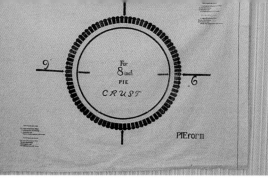

Above: A piecrust blueprint outlined on an old linen dish towel, $4 from Sage Street Antiques, Sag Harbor, New York, hangs in Ellen's kitchen art exhibition.

The warmest and most personal place to entertain is in the kitchen. Guests naturally seem to gravitate there. If you plan a prewedding breakfast or brunch—a kitchen shower would be perfect—liven things up by setting your table with some of your favorite old cookbooks (see one of Ellen's at right). You could, if you're in a generous mood, give a different edition to each of your guests or have *them* bring one for the bride-to-be! (For more on vintage cookbooks, see page 18.)

Right: *The American Everyday Cookbook*, by Agnes Murphy, published by Random House in 1955, a birthday gift from Ellen's friend Wayne.
Opposite: It's the apron that matches the cookbook, at right, the tablecloth, the floor, the vintage pileup of linens in the dining room. It's the apron the only woman in America who still loves to wash dishes by hand could possibly wear. "It's ruffled and bibbed. I look like a fool wearing it, but I'm dry!" Ellen O'Neill laughs. Its home is the latch on the cupboard door, another built-in, to the right of the stove. "Yes," she sighs, "it's another blue-and-white manifestation." To clean old aprons, see Lisa Durfee's tips on page 37; to launder old linens, see Ellen's advice at right.

HOW TO LAUNDER OLD LINENS

It might have been Ellen O'Neill's two great-aunts, who both ran dress shops in the 1940s, who started her on the road to loving old textiles. Most table linens of the dish-towel, napkin, and tablecloth variety can probably be thrown right into the washing machine with Clorox 2 and detergent on the gentle cycle. For those pieces that can't withstand the agitation of a washing machine, like fragile batiste, things with lace trim and insets, and very sheer fabrics, boiling them on top of the stove with bleach is a safer alternative. Here are Ellen's tips:

- Fill a big roasting pan with water and Snowy bleach (to determine the exact amount, read the directions on the box) and bring to a boil on top of the stove.
- Reduce heat to a simmer and submerge your linens with a long-handled wooden spoon. (I keep one just for that purpose, and a special pan too.) Let simmer for ten minutes, stirring occasionally. The boiling separates the fibers. The bleach bubbles the dirt through. (This is a speedier process than the soaking for-a-couple-of-days method.) Carefully empty into a deep sink or tub and run under lukewarm water (cold water shrinks the fabric). Towel dry and fold into white plastic garbage bags and refrigerate for at least an hour and up to a week. Iron them right out of the refrigerator. They're slightly stiff, so no starch is necessary. Heavier items may require steam or spraying with water. They'll smell wonderfully hygienic.
- For really tough stains, Ellen has discovered Z'Out, a concentrated stain remover. The Vermont Country Store carries this through its catalog. The phone number is (802) 362-2400 (no collect calls please). The address: Vermont Country Store, Mail Order Office, P.O. Box 3000, Manchester Center, VT 05255-3000.

the blues

Joan Baez crooned the attributes of a dog named Blue back in the 1960s. Joni Mitchell's song and album *Blue*, released in 1971, is still the most haunting musical blue. But for my friend Mark Campbell (you met him earlier in "Sinking Spells," pages 48–59) blue is what he wants to drink out of (his dogs too; see the bowl above), eat on, see piled up in his cupboards, set on his tables, and spread over his lap. The hunt for blue pottery, glassware, linens, table mats, food screens, dog bowls, coffee urns, teapots, bowls, creamers, plates, platters, and everything in between began years ago at the weekly Twenty-sixth Street Flea Market, in New York City. On the West Coast it was the Rose Bowl, the monthly flea in Pasadena. Back in New York it was trips to the landmark shop of kitchenalia, Kitschen, on Bleecker Street, and, it goes without saying, every yard and tag sale, auction, estate sale, and thrift shop singing his kind of blues.

Beach house blues lined up in the light of day. Back row from left to right: Dark blue plate, unmarked, from Twenty-sixth Street Flea Market, New York City, $25; a Catalina charger (rare) from the Rose Bowl, Pasadena, California, $50; an Ultra-California Pottery Company, Vernon Kilns, found at Twenty-sixth Street Flea, for $20. Middle row left to right: An unmarked (possibly Fiesta ware) wooden-handled ceramic coffeepot from Kitschen, New York City, $12.50; an unmarked but more than likely Fiesta ware water pitcher from a yard sale for $6; a pale blue green teapot marked "USA LaHaska" from the Twenty-sixth Street Flea for $10; a vintage syrup pitcher with drip catcher, unmarked, from Lambertville, New Jersey, for $10. Front row left to right: Sky blue creamer by Caribe, made in the USA, from Twenty-sixth Street Flea for $5; toucan pitcher, made in Japan, from Kitschen, for $12; a pale blue pitcher made by Shenansago from Twenty-sixth Street Flea for $5; a Fiesta ware creamer from Kitschen; a nest of custard bowls—some Fiesta, some unmarked—all from the Twenty-sixth Street Flea.

Though the artist in residence at Mark Campbell's seaside kitchen table is Henri Matisse, it is Pierre Bonnard whom I think of when I study the table composition closely. Possibly I'm overly swayed by the anticipation of a new show of his work opening the next day at the Museum of Modern Art because with the exception of the little vase of frothy roses, this setting couldn't be more like a Bonnard breakfast table. Study *The Breakfast Table*, painted in 1936, which pictures the small sitting room of his little pink stucco house on a hill in Le Cannet, near Cannes. Though the table is set with only a few items—a large teapot, cups and saucers, a plate, and assorted containers—it is a patchwork of vivid color and texture. I dream of his arrival at Mark's table with his plate-palette in hand and wish my photographs could capture the still beauty of this table with the same explosion of texture and ecstatic color I know his paintbrush would bring.

The swirls of pink, blue, and yellow encircling the vintage glass pitcher and matching glasses mimic both the colors of the Lu-Ray dishes collected piecemeal for about $5 to $10 each from the Twenty-sixth Street Flea Market, New York City, and the set of vintage place mats picked up for $5 from Kitschen, New York City. Pink lemonade is waiting in the wings.

In the more informal atmosphere of today's workplace, water is served up in those ubiquitous plastic bottles, and lattes and cappuccinos (rarely just ordinary coffee) are sipped out of dome-topped paper cups. In the 1940s and 1950s, depending upon your rung on the executive ladder, you might have had one of these chunky little stainless urns to keep you company and refreshed with either hot or cold libations. Mark Campbell has collected them for years, preferring those painted blue or green and topped with the classic mercury glass stoppers as those seen second and third from the left. He scooped up most of these, popular from the 1930s through the 1950s, in the 1980s and 90s, from a range of $15 to $30. I spotted a pink one the other day for $45 and walked away.

Opposite: According to Mark Campbell, antique food screens are not so hard to find. The problem is finding them in good shape. Rust weakens the fragile screening and eventually causes it to become vulnerable to punctures and separations. Mark suggests spraying them once or twice a season with Mop & Glo. "You'd be amazed at how effective it is in inhibiting rust," Mark attests. Most of Mark's screens were collected at the Pier and Coliseum antique shows held annually in New York City. The three stacked on the left were $55; the smaller one on the back row right was around $10. Used to protect meat and other food from flies, the originals, produced from the late 1870s to the 1950s, were made not only of wire but also of muslin. They're still as vital today "especially," puts in Mark, "in a beach house without screen doors or for an open-air picnic."

Left: The first seltzer bottle I can recall was the one that Clarabell, the clown, used to torment Buffalo Bob and the young studio audience on *The Howdy Doody Show*. Water under pressure spritzed out an effervescent bubbly version that could zing you far better than a child's water gun. The blue glass version belongs to Sam Hamilton, a collector whose kitchen wares are on pages 204–5. It is reminiscent of the kind delivered to households in the 1940s and 1950s. A spritz of bubbly seltzer into a glass with Fox's U-Bet chocolate syrup produced an official plain chocolate soda. If you added milk to it, it was an egg cream. In the 1950s you could go to the local drugstore and it could spritz up an egg cream in a jiffy. With the demise of the soda counter you have to fend for yourself. For years we fended by ordering a wooden case of those great blue bottles from Gimme Seltzer. Seltzer bottles are a unique and international collectible. I just brought one with a turquoise metal jacket back from a flea market in Buenos Aires for $10.

This is the story of how one great find no matter how small or how extravagant can inspire you (when you get it home) to relook at everything you have and to rethink the way it lives and the story it tells in your home. That's what happened the day Bobby Ball was a volunteer worker at American Junk, the flagship store of junk that my sister Nell and I opened the summer of 1997 in White Stone, Virginia. While he was sifting through junk, a green graniteware roasting pan, seen at right, caught Bobby's eye. "It was a little pricey at $24," he admits, but because of his good service in the store that day he "got off like a bandit. . . ." That's when the story gets really good. As Bobby tells it, "I went right home and did my kitchen over with the roaster as the focal point." He painted the cupboard a dark gray called "nocturnal forest" and edged it with a pinky red and white stripe. Bobby's green roaster "will be perfect," he insists, "for baking wild duck, wild goose, and a turkey at Thanksgiving," but more than the meals to come, he can thank it for inspiring a whole new kitchen.

Right: Surrounding Bobby's green roasting pan are old cookware friends. The blue Ball jars behind it were used for putting up fresh sausage and hog fat. The grater above was for grating cheese, especially good on pear and peach salad. If too rusty, Bobby suggests using them as a unique light shade. Screw cup hooks in the ceiling around the bulb and hang four or five around it. The old granite colander above it he found in a barn for a $1. The copper pot to its left was very popular with the kids because it was the best for making fudge and taffy.

Born in the 1800s, graniteware was basically thin sheets of iron, steel, or aluminum coated with enamel. Not only did it translate to cookware that was practical, affordable, and easy to care for, but for the first time the housewife could enjoy a whole range of colors to choose from. Graniteware surfaces were solid, speckled (like the colander hanging at right), marbleized, and streaked. During the Depression most graniteware companies closed down, and the new darling of housewives became aluminum cookware. A revival of graniteware began in the 1950s, which is more than likely the date of this blue speckled pot. I found it sans lid at a tag sale for $1.50. In the warmer months it lives outdoors with a cargo of blooming geraniums.

Turn back to page 34 and remember the vintage textile tales of Lisa Durfee. When she and her partner Michael bought the 1850s ginger-bread-trimmed cottage in the Hudson Valley surrounded by apple orchards and mountain views, she was more than satisfied. Little did she know that even more treasures awaited her on the inside, buried behind her kitchen walls. Her story below.

WALLPAPER: A LOVE STORY

When we bought this old house, its interior was like a step back into 1949. Its previous owner, Edna House, was an avid gardener and had wallpapered every room in fabulous florals: roses in the living room, honeysuckle in the east bedroom, apple blossoms in the west, etc. Sadly, the kitchen and dining room walls had been covered over in 1980s vinyls. I could hear the old paper calling out to me from underneath. My tricky task was to soak and peel off the new paper and leave the old hanging. I succeeded and was rewarded with a trellis-and-ivy motif in the kitchen (see opposite page) and chartreuse magnolias in the dining room (at left). The bad news was that it was indeed in very rough shape, even for a distressed-look junkie like me. The incredible news was that Edna, God bless her soul, had saved all the scraps and extra rolls of old wallpaper and had tucked them neatly away in the loft of the barn. Some of them were still wrapped in their original Montgomery Ward brown paper and string. Almost fifty years later I was (painstakingly) able to rehang the whole dining room and most of the kitchen. Of course it was worth it—even if I have to bite my tongue when the occasional visitor asks, "So, what are you going to do about this old kitchen?"

Above: Lisa Durfee's choice of dish detergent is based on how well the container fits into her little blue graniteware pot.

Right: It is the extraordinary shelf valance embroidered with the tools of the kitchen that sets the tone and the palette for Lisa's picture-perfect collection of blue and green containers stacked and packed into the vintage shelves that were part of the charm of the 1850s kitchen she cannot love enough. It was $1, evidence she believes that dealers do make deals. More evidence: the silver prom queen statuette marked $25 but hers for $3. (Lisa, tell us your secret . . . please!) The green enamel fridge dishes under the queen were $2 each at Rinaldi's Flea Market, Pleasant Valley, New York. The milk glass salt shaker was a $2 yard sale capture. The four-piece daisy-clad canister set on the top shelf, far right, was $2 at Thriftique, Millerton, New York.

Opposite: The rewards of Lisa's painstaking wallpaper restoration (read the love story, opposite) are captured in this view from the kitchen to the dining room. The dining room doubles as kitchen nook with a picket fence motif enamel-top table, $22 at a local auction. The four wooden slat-back chairs were $35 at another one. The green vase at center, a $2 piece of McCoy pottery, holds a 25-cent fake cat o' nines. The lotus vase to its left was $1. The $4 ﬁgure in the corner is an iron, make-believe Buddha. The little bridge on the windowsill adds yet another Asian touch, as do the paint-by-number masterpieces collected at tag sales for a few dollars.

Zoom in on the prized center-piece of Lisa's tabletop land-scape: plastic beaded fruit, picked from bountiful tag sale tables for $2 and nested into a $1 bowl. The dogwood napkins matching the wallpaper were $1 for the four. The little teapot holder came with the house. The fallen leaves (from plastic trees!), seasonal coasters for cups of hot cider, were raked up for a nickel each.

plastic makes perfect

f I had been a housewife in the mid-1930s, when plastic kitchenware was introduced, I might have started a small revolution. It was the Depression. Every penny counted. Rubbermaid's first semisynthetic rubber dustpan cost $1. A normal metal one cost 39 cents. (You can guess what my choice would have been!) Even though plastics offered the housewife all kinds of value, utility, and style for her kitchen, it wasn't until the late 1940s, after World War II, that the new miracle stuff got better and cheaper and started to live up to some of its promises. Today I look around my kitchen and see plastic spatulas, coffee measures, a plastic pitcher of juice in the fridge. This summer I had my own kind of Tupperware party (you're invited on the opposite page), setting a whole table with plastic fantastics in all shades of romantic pastels. I guess you could say I've made my peace with plastic.

Above: Jerry Pontes, a collector, surfer, and artist who turns his dreams of the South Seas into watery landscapes, sea goddesses, and glimpses of sand-strewn paradises, for lack of a canvas turned to the largest blank space available in his seafaring hideaway on the Outer Banks of North Carolina, his General Electric refrigerator, and brought his fantasy island home to the kitchen.

Preceding pages: Celebrating the Golden Age of Plastic Dinnerware, 1947 to 1955, a sampler table of the some of the best and worst! On the far left: a pair of pale yellow bowls bottom-stamped with the Aztec sun, a brand by Molmac, picked up for $3 at Cookin' in San Francisco. The first two of the five picnic-style divided plates seen on the table are from the Gorhamware line made in the United States. The other three, unstamped, were part of a set of five. All were 15 cents each at The Rummage Shoppe, Millerton, New York. The smiling plastic pitcher for the classic summer refresher Kool-Aid, $8, from The Twila Zone, Nags Head, North Carolina. A set of icy colored coasters to cradle those icy tumblers of tea, $1, from The Rummage Shoppe. The pistachio-colored Texas Ware bowl and the pottery fish trivet were $3 each at Cookin'. The pastel ice cube trays were 25 cents each from Penny Paid, Locust Hill, Virginia. The plastic cutlery is stored in a Texas Ware speckled bowl, $9.75, Cookin'. The lighthouse ashtray, which once held a hefty bottle of Jim Beam, cost me $12 at a tag sale.

Left: Plastics set the scene (a seafaring one) and the table (a blue Formica-topped one) in my carriage house loft in upstate New York. The closest water is the stream that runs down the mountain and cuts through our land, not more than fifty feet away from this less than shipshape structure. Nonetheless, the captain has hung her hat and crab net (see them in the left corner) and has stuck a candle in a bottle that might have floated down our stream with a message scrawled on a piece of plastic bag: "Help! I'm a prisoner in a plastic life!"

Earl Tupper was born in 1907. He grew up on a farm in Harvard, Massachusetts. He was shy and retiring. In today's vernacular, he would have been described as a genius nerd. You might have seen him on the cover of *Fortune* with the likes of Bill Gates. In 1940 he went to work as a chemical engineer for the Du Pont company. He loved to play with a thermoplastic slag that Du Pont named polyethylene. It was a kind of a superplastic, resistant to chemicals and freezing temperatures, tasteless, odorless, buoyant. In 1942 Tupper left Du Pont and started the Tupper Plastics Company. He took a few tons of polyethylene with him. Du Pont was happy to give him as much as he wanted. He invented Poly-T, short for Polyethylene Tupper, a plastic that didn't split and was durable enough to withstand almost any form of abuse. During World War II Earl used it to create gas masks and Navy signal lamp parts. But 1946 was Earl's claim-to-fame year. Using injection molding he began to create household storage and utility containers with a unique and indispensable airtight feature. There were tumblers, canisters, bowls. Tupperware was born. The Tupperware parties (my version on page 150) came after sales foundered in stores. The gospel of Tupperware needed plastic evangelists to explain the unique features of each item. It wasn't long before they came, invited, partied, and sold! The word of Tupperware has converted house-wives from the 1940s up until now.

A chorus line of colorful plastic cups swooped up in one swell swoop at The Rummage Shoppe, Millerton, New York. The Tupperware tumblers to the far left were 50 cents each. The orange and blue juice cups were made in the USA, but are not Earl's stuff. The next to last is SparkleWare, and the itsy-bitsy pink is (I don't believe it! I assumed this was a cough medicine measurer, but upon inspecting the bottom, I see it bears the royal stamp of Tupperware) a plastic shot! Earl, you amaze!

Six coasters in search of tall Tupperware tumblers to complement and cradle. (You saw them on the previous page.) They personify cool. Tupperware's icy pastel slivers of transparent plastic sandwich a pad of absorbent paper between two layers of plastic. The top layer is pricked with tiny holes to drain the cool sweat of the tumblers. Plastic perfection for $1 (the price was too good to be true, so I left it on) from The Rummage Shoppe, Millerton, New York.

It was a typical August day on the Outer Banks of North Carolina, hot and muggy. But at four o'clock in the afternoon, as I drove along the Beach Highway, the ocean to my left, the sun setting over the far dunes on my right, it was nothing less than brilliant. My state of mind was like the day: maybe not brilliant but certainly elated as I turned the car into The Twila Zone, one of my favorite junking haunts along the Virginia Dare Trail. I waved to Jo-Lee, the owner, and motioned that I was headed around back to the garage she had converted into a space for oversize pieces. When I saw the scene at right, just inside the doorway, I couldn't help myself. The mundane metal rocker cushioned in yellow plastic cradled a symphony of pastel hues so romantic that I actually fell in love with plastic that day.

Right: The objects of my affection: the frosted pink candy tray that reminded me of my favorite lipstick shade in the early 1960s, was $1; the pastel watercolor underneath was a gift from Jo-Lee; the yellow basket weave polyethylene serving basket with a pull-out blue divider tray inside was $1 (down-home restaurants and diners still serve fried chicken dinners in them). The large red wallpaper blossom is attached to the inside of a picture frame back. I bought it for 50 cents. The stack of Melmac cups and saucers was $5.

Opposite: A still life worthy of Bonnard, arranged on a rick-rack rainbow striped apron, $3.50, from D's Place at Holland's Stage Coach Markets, Gloucester, Virginia. The pair of turquoise mugs, probably from a picnic set, was manufactured by Colonial Plastics, Cleveland, Ohio, sometime in the 1950s. The Texas Ware cups were $3 each at Cookin', San Francisco. The two plastic plates were 15 cents each from The Rummage Shoppe, Millerton, New York.

got no milk

Nine children drank a lot of milk. My first recollection of its delivery was in Richmond, when my mother heard from our milkman that one of our neighbors hadn't received his butter for several weeks. It turned out, after some sleuthing that it was our St. Bernard, who would ride along in the milkman's truck, watch as butter was dropped off at the neighbor's, and return later to gobble it down box, paper, and all. Some years later, when we moved to the Northern Neck of Virginia, my parents installed a milk machine; bottles or cartons didn't do the job anymore. Our milkman, Mac Haynie, always got a chuckle out of bringing that big box of milk to our door. His daughter Helen Jean was one of my best friends, and the day we opened American Junk, in White Stone, Virginia, she came to wish us luck and brought a glass milk bottle from her father's dairy. It looks a lot like one of those seen in the carrier on pages 160–61.

Preceding pages: Got no milk (and no milk mustache either!) in my six quart milk bottles. Each is embossed with the Borden Eagle brand trademark and a big "Property of Borden's Condensed Milk Co." My friend Alice Reid picked up these six and a lot more at George Cole Auctioneers, Red Hook, New York, for $3 each. She snagged the typical milk bottle holder separately at another Cole auction for $10. The golden age of glass milk bottles was from 1910 to 1950. Alice's are probably from the 1940s.

Above: Got milk in one of a trio of half pints I picked off a shelf at the SoHo Flea Market, New York City, for $2 each. The portrait of the cow, not Elsie but a sturdier type, sends the comforting message "Direct from Farm to You." I use this one to pour milk for coffee or syrup for pancakes.
Opposite: In Stephen Drucker's *Life* magazine 1948 kitchen it is not surprising to find glass milk bottles complete with their perfectly preserved caps. Painted bottles or pyro-glazed replaced embossing and date a bottle as later.

When milk containers went plastic in the 1950s, so did the carriers. This green one from a local dairy in upstate New York was $2 at a tag sale in the area. My husband stores his collection of 78s in it.

FITCHETT BROS.
DAIRY
POUGHKEEPSIE, N.Y. 1-75

Above: Strong, Maine (and I rely on my friend Alice Reid for the geographical references here), is in the midsection of Maine, near the western lakes area. Alice has a yen to move to Maine, but not necessarily to Strong. So, when she saw the milk bottle sign for Allen's Dairy, to her it was a signpost to Maine. She discovered it at the Brimfield Market, Brimfield, Massachusetts, and paid about $30 for it.

Left: The golden age of the glass milk bottle lasted about forty years—from 1910 to 1950. The first paper carton appeared in the early 1920s and 1930s, but it wasn't until 1950 that it really took hold. Krim-Ko Chocolate Flavored Drink was pasteurized at the Chula Vista Dairy in Eugene, Oregon, probably around that time. It was a gift sent to me by a photographer and collector, Joshua Greene, who lives out that way. The little violet-covered glass beside it could be a Swankyswig, those decorated glass containers that came filled with Kraft cheese spreads starting in the early 1930s. Though it's hard to say if my little chocolate milk glass qualifies, I could swear my olfactory system picks up the faintest scent of cheese when I bring it up to my mouth to take a sip. I bought it at Northeast Antiques, Millerton, New York, for $2. The color-coordinated green hot plate beneath it, from Cookin' in San Francisco, was $3. The embroidered pouch of potholders behind them was $8, from Tomorrow's Treasures, Pleasant Valley, New York.

Right: I have always wanted to paint. Instead I write about painters whom I love, take pictures of their works of art, and collect as much as I can. Of course I have no Matisses or Bonnards on my walls. Most of my canvases are signed, but by no one you'd know. I discover them at tag sales and auctions for a few dollars—$15 at most. I collect portraits of people, still lifes of flowers and fruit, landscapes, but no cows. When my sister Cary started painting four years ago, I was very impressed and just a little jealous. Last summer on our annual summer family holiday she began this one of two cows in a field with a wonderful slightly dilapidated house in the background. She calls it "cow-work-in-progress," an oil on canvas, August 1997. I call it moo-ving.

Opposite: When the cows get up, I'm up too, hunting for junk. On April 12, 1997, I followed a winding road to a tag sale I had spotted just a few miles from our farm. I was an "early bird" (term for those annoying junkers who arrive earlier than the tag sale is advertised to begin), which is how I walked away with this reproduction of a painting. It was nicely framed and in good condition so I didn't feel too bad plunking down the two tens. I put it up in our barn. (Where else to put a cow?) On July 2 it was trucked down to American Junk, our store in White Stone, Viriginia, where it was reserved the night before we officially opened. We granted this privilege to Mary and Jim McDaniels, owners of The River Market, a neighboring establishment (diagonally across the street), who had stopped by to bring us some late-night sustenance as we (the entire Carter family doing a Christmas Eve kind of all nighter!) frantically finished the last one hundred details for our junk store opening on the Fourth of July.

Above: When people are looking for our farm, we tell them to look for the black-and-white cow that guards the entrance of our carriage house. My sons, Carter and Sam, brought her home at the end of the spring school term seven years ago and plopped her right where she's stood since then. She's a hefty bovine, 3 feet by almost 8 feet, an abandoned art project by a departing senior.

Left: Robert Carter Ball, known as Bobby, is a friend and relative with a great eye (you've seen the results of that on pages 56 and 144) and lots of friends who love to send him things they know "only he" will appreciate. Case in point, the framed portrait of a black-and-white cow (he thinks a Holstein) sent as a gift. Normally it hangs in his kitchen, grouped with ancestral portraits (he has a sense of humor too), but for the summer it has moved to the porch to commingle with more kindred spirits: an old crab net, pitchfork, and stepladder from the barn.

Opposite, clockwise from top: 1. A cool place for a Canadian cow, on top of our refrigerator in the kitchen at Elm Glen Farm. It was a gift to me from my husband, Howard, bought in one of those big antique shops that, according to him, I'd never go in. Above it hangs a drawing of a former residence created by Carter when he was eight. **2.** A bovine bonnet and decorative china spoon from Kitty Hawk Thrift, Consignment and Antiques, Kitty Hawk, North Carolina, for 00 and $1, respectively. **3.** Two mugs udderly tasteless and unattractive, but I couldn't resist the 50 cents' commitment at a Saturday tag sale in Dutchess County, New York.

tin pan alley

Every New Year's Eve, as the clock struck twelve, my sisters and brothers, led by our mother and father, would grab pots and pans and march outside, beating them like drums with wooden spoons, wire whisks, and heavy-duty enamel spoons. It was our kind of celebratory tin pan music—loud, noisy, and totally out of tune. It was in some ways close to the derivation of the meaning of tin pan music used in the early 1900s to decry music that was thought to be cheap, everyday, and very commercial. Tin Pan Alley referred to the district where tin pan music was composed and published. My collection of tin canisters, cookie tins, and cake savers, seen at left and on the following pages, would serve a full tin pan orchestra.

Above: Cookie tins are easy to find and cheap to collect. Because they are so plenteous, it is a good idea to focus on one decorative theme. I chose flowers. The four blooming on the top shelf were gathered at The Carriage Factory Antique Center, Flint, New York, for $1.50 each. The cake saver, below left, from The Twila Zone, Nags Head, North Carolina, is one of a pair decorated with a Pennsylvania Dutch design. This larger, more standard size cost $12. The smaller of the pair, seen on the bottom shelf in the picture at left, was a unique 9" x 4" size for $10. The tin to the right decorated with a watercolor by the Swedish artist Carl Larsson (if you own *Garden Junk* review his story on page 9) was picked up for $3 from The Rummage Shoppe, Millerton, New York.

Left: Though I focus on floral cookie tins and canisters, I couldn't resist the trio of Christmas Scottie tins in graduated sizes collected at a Copake Auction, Copake, New York, tag sale for $1. The smallest crowns the top of a stack resting on a red metal kitchen stool, $5, from The Twila Zone. The other two are seen on the shelf to its right. Turn the page for a full view of the collection.

Clockwise from right: 1. In New York City the home of Tin Pan Alley is the Brill Building at 1619 Broadway. At Elm Glen Farm the equivalent is my skyscraper six-shelf cupboard rising five feet nine inches from the rough hand-hewn boards of our carriage house. It is a version of a pie safe with wire-fronted doors that I dug out of Alice Reid's barn in Livingston, New York. It cost more than my whole tin collection—$250. The farmstand Golden Corn sign propped on top and the timothy grain bag draped over the door at right were part of a box lot for $15 at George Cole Auctioneers, Red Hook, New York. Top shelf highlights: The two wooden dolls were $9 at Shoestring Antiques & Gallery, Norfolk, Connecticut; the little green sink between them was a gift with the cupboard from Alice Reid. The two canisters on either side of the dolls were $4 for the one on the left, $12.50 for the one on the right, from Cookin', San Francisco. The toy metal cupboard and sink set below, were picked up at Fredie's Shack, Geneva, New York, for $35. **2.** Stocking the toy kitchen cupboard, at left, is a counterful of miniature-size foodstuffs. **3.** Inventory of a $15 Cole Auctioneers box lot bid: the linen timothy grain bag, a brand-new L. L. Bean blanket, another linen grain bag, plus the Golden Corn sign. **4.** It was the geranium sugar decal that made this canister a have-to-have for $4 at Cookin'. **5.** Most canister sets were designed with four matching containers that nested inside one another when not in use. Flour, sugar, coffee, and tea were the main contents. These two with handwritten designations were a quarter apiece at a yard sale table. Of the pair of decorated metal recipe boxes, the one on the top was definitely the bargain: 20 cents from a tag sale. The one below, from Northeast Antiques, Millerton, New York, with recipe card separators included, was $4. Most house standard 3" x 5" recipe cards and offer a unique organizational system for the cook. Kitchen computers may one day make them obsolete. **6.** It had to be for Christmas cookies, this cozy illustrated tin keeper, $1 from D's Place at Holland's Stage Coach Markets, Gloucester, Virginia. **7.** An enameled tinware canister decorated with decals was $2 at The Rummage Shoppe, Millerton, New York. In the 1920s a six-piece set like this would have cost about 79 cents.

There is no traffic noise outside Mark Campbell's seaside kitchen. If you pause and listen, what you might hear is the pounding surf or hummingbirds hovering in the flower garden just beyond the kitchen's doorstep. It is not only the simplest and most romantic of kitchens (visited earlier on pages 48–49 and 134–43) but the most productive. There is rarely a time when someone, whether Mark or his housemate, John, or a visiting weekend guest, isn't up to some kind of culinary delight. On my first visit there, I was greeted with the sweet smell of a freshly baked pound cake being prepared for lunch. The collection of vintage tin cake and bread boxes at right were designed to store and save what might be leftover cake. Today Mark uses them mostly to store excess flour and pasta and small baking tools and tins.

Right: Mark's twin towers of vintage cake bins, canisters, keepers, and bread boxes. All came at one time or another from the Twenty-sixth Street Flea Market, New York City, for $5 to $15. Though the shapes and responsibilities differ, the uniform shades of pale green and cream build team spirit.

Opposite: Mrs. Ball's pie and cake tins displayed on the back porch at Hurstville. On the top shelf, the lemon pie pans. The one on the right was perforated, according to Bobby, "so the crust wouldn't sweat." Bobby endorses this old wooden rolling pin and Flako piecrust for the thinnest piecrust ever. On the second shelf are the Ball family cake pans, circa 1930. The cutter blades help remove the cake more easily. Below the baking tins is an original Mrs. Smith's pie pan.

Bobby Ball lives in a early frame dormered house called Hurstville located in the Northern Neck of Virginia. Until a few years ago he shared it with Mrs. Ball, his mother. They both enjoyed a good game of bridge and good home cooking. Mrs. Ball often relied on *The Reedville Cook Book* (her well-worn copy can be seen on page 177). Having hailed from Colorado, she was much more familiar with the preparation of beef than seafood. What Bobby particularly remembers is his mother's lemon pie, which he still bakes (see the recipe on the next page) using the same pie tins she did, seen at left. "We always lived with old junk. Some things were from a generation before. We became attached to them and never bought the new-fangled products of the day—except old/new things from a farm sale." Revisit some of Bobby's old/new things in his kitchen on page 144.

**BE TOUGH ON RUST:
DON'T LINGER IN THE WATER**

The reason Bobby Ball can still count on his family's baking tins that date back to the 1930s is that they took good care of them. If you plan to use any early tin, steel, or cast-iron baking ware, don't let it soak too long in the water or it'll rust. Wash carefully, wipe immediately with a clean towel, and store in a dry place.

Recipe: *Lemon Pie*
From: *Mrs. Thomas Francis Ball, Sr. (Bayview)* Makes: *9 inch pie*
(One 9 inch baked pie crust)

3 eggs
1 cup of sugar
3 teasp. cold water
1 - Lemon

Beat yolks of 3 eggs with ½ cup sugar
Add 3 teaspoons of water
Add the juice of one lemon / grate the rind and add —
(Cook this mixture in a double boiler until thick —

©CURRENT INC., COLORADO SPRINGS, CO 80941

Above: Mrs. Ball's lemon pie recipe resting in one of the pair of pie pans she always baked them in. Bobby still makes two, as she always did. One is never enough. He warns that if you like lemon meringue pie, you might be disappointed. This one is soft, a version of lemon chess pie. It needs a very thin, flaky crust. "Melts in your mouth."

Above right: A handwritten recipe for butterscotch refrigerator cookies tucked into Mrs. Ball's well-used copy of *The Reedville Cook Book*. "Every home in Northumberland and Lancaster counties had a Bible and *The Reedville Cook Book*," attests Bobby.

Below Right: Regional cookbooks are fun to collect not only for the recipes, but for what they reveal about the cooks and the history of the area. *Favorite Recipes*, November 6, 1931, is a very personal collection I picked up in The Second Hand Shop, Geneva, New York, for 50 cents.

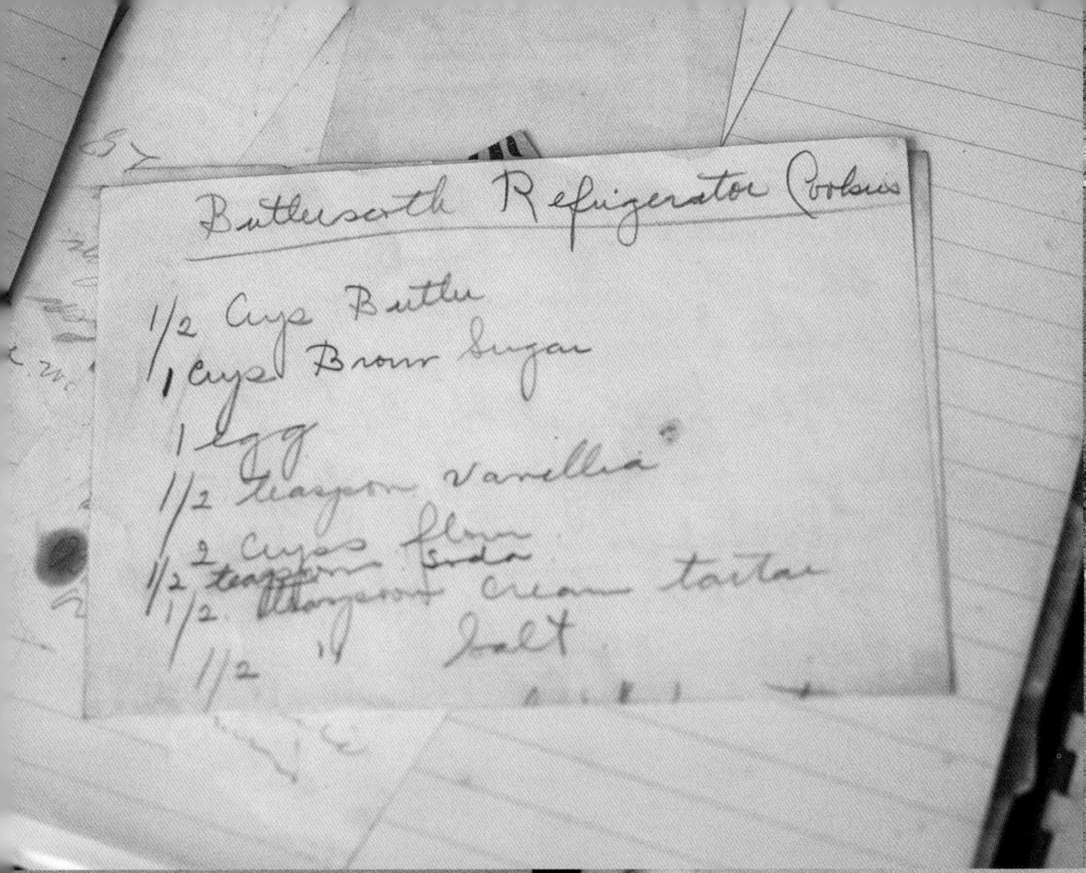

Butterscotch Refrigerator Cookies

1/2 Cups Butter
1 Cups Brown Sugar
1 Egg
1/2 Teaspoon Vanilla
2 Cups flour
1/2 teaspoon soda
1/2 teaspoon Cream tartar
1/2 " Salt

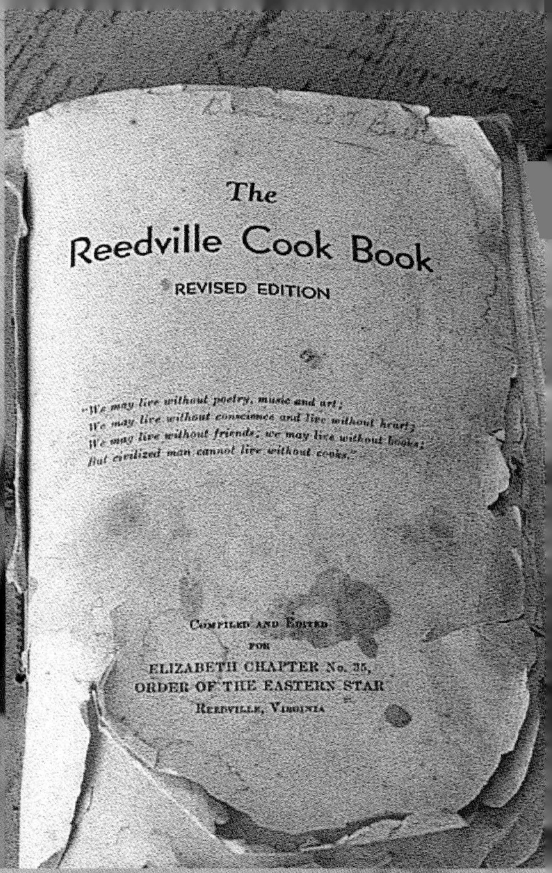

The Reedville Cook Book

REVISED EDITION

"We may live without poetry, music and art;
We may live without conscience and live without heart;
We may live without friends; we may live without books;
But civilized man cannot live without cooks."

COMPILED AND EDITED
FOR
ELIZABETH CHAPTER No. 35,
ORDER OF THE EASTERN STAR
REEDVILLE, VIRGINIA

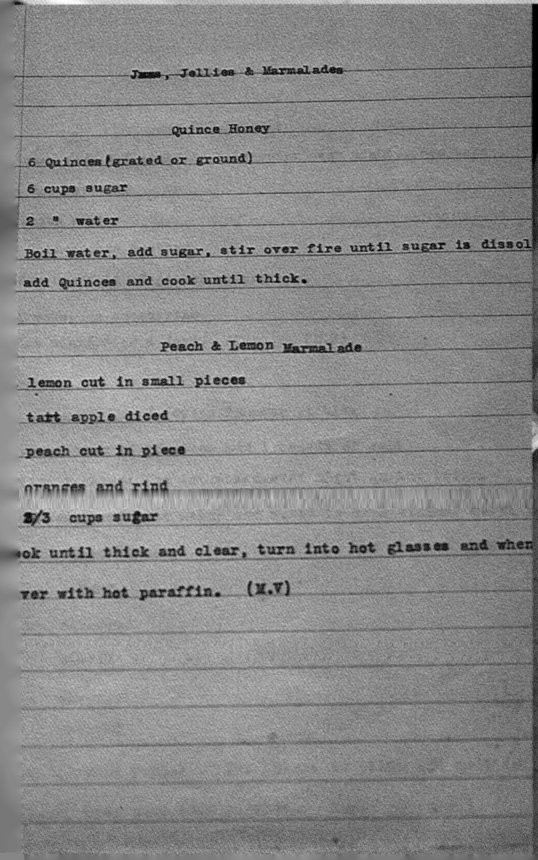

Jams, Jellies & Marmalades

Quince Honey

6 Quinces (grated or ground)
6 cups sugar
2 " water
Boil water, add sugar, stir over fire until sugar is dissol
add Quinces and cook until thick.

Peach & Lemon Marmalade

lemon cut in small pieces
tart apple diced
peach cut in piece
oranges and rind
3/3 cups sugar
ok until thick and clear, turn into hot glasses and when
ver with hot paraffin. (M.V)

Favorite Recipes
Copyright November 6, 1931.

Above: One way to get knives off a crowded kitchen counter is to get a wall-mounted knife rack like the one I found for $3 (including the knives!) at a Copake Auction tag sale, Copake, New York.

In the Middle Ages bread was hung from the ceilings in large wooden frames called bread flakes. This wasn't an exercise in storage efficiency, just a way to keep the mice and rats at bay. By the mid-nineteenth century bread was brought down to earth and stored in earthenware lidded crocks. In the nineteenth century stoneware crocks were introduced, and in the twentieth century bread bins of enameled iron were it! Keeping bread well ventilated has always been a challenge. Kitchen furniture, popular at the turn of the century, often contained metal-lined bread drawers. When these pieces became outmoded, the decorative bread box took off.

I love bread boxes. Most of mine are the conventional hinged lift-up-top variety like the one seen at top left. My favorite, picked up a few years back at the Georgetown Flea Market in Washington, D.C., has a red top and a perfect corncob on the side. It cost about $12. The problem is that it doesn't have enough ventilation holes and has spoiled more bread than it has saved. Be sure when buying bread bins that they are properly ventilated. If not, do what I do, and use them to store nonperishable things like letters, magazine articles, small books, and, as Mark Campbell suggested on page 174, cutlery or small kitchen tools. I display my country collection on a high shelf in our carriage house, along with assorted metal lunch boxes. (See *American Junk*, page 92.)

Top left: A hinged lift-top bread box decorated with a frieze of teapots and kitchenware. It beckoned from a yard sale in Virginia for $3. If you plan on using these boxes for alternative storage, consider spray painting a top like this one that is a little funky.

Bottom left: This bread box has two doors and two storage compartments. It's a little bent out of shape but I bought it nonetheless, for the color and the whimsical decal. It was a quarter at an upstate New York yard sale. Its bread years have passed. Now it stores jars of nails, staples, and miscellaneous small tools.

Opposite: A 1930s English enameled bread bin in Carol Levison's kitchen in Massachusetts. The problem, as Carol sees it, is that English bread boxes aren't "junk." She has seen them priced for upward of $100, depending on their color and condition. They are rapidly vanishing in England, so the value and demand are escalating. Solutions: (1) Call Carol, and try to make a deal (she does have them and sells them from Once Upon a Table, Pittsfield, Massachusetts, see Junk Guide); (2) go to England and try your luck; (3) collect the more popular American versions seen at left.

179

Memorial Day weekend 1997. It is the tag sale weekend of all weekends, and I'm ready. There is a "huge barn sale" in Hillsdale, New York, a three-family yard sale just west of there, and 1.2 miles south of it an ex-collector is selling everything! I know all this because I've done my homework. I have combed the local shoppers' guides and newspaper for all the tag sales in the area. I've noted the ones that sound intriguing and arranged them by starting time and geography. How'd I do? Check my tally below and the booty, at right.

Above, clockwise from top: 1. Metal containers were first used to package goods in the United States in the early 1800s. This little chorus line of three baking powders, three Durkee's spices, and two jars of Musterole were a package deal, including the pure ground spices box, for $8 at Elephant's Trunk Bazaar, New Milford, Connecticut. **2.** A 5-pound net weight Shedd's peanut butter can was a kitchen junk present from my friend and the art director of this book, Tracy Monahan! **3.** A 12-ounce Ritz crackers can, dated 1982, was $3 at Americana Collectibles, Hudson, New York. See it in its new home on page 10. **4.** A trio of peanut butter cans at Alice Reid's Antiques in the Barn, Livingston, New York.

kitchen aids

One of the most popular flour sifters, according to one of my kitchen collectibles research books, is this 1950s Androck Hand-I-Sift. Carol Levison is the lucky owner. She paid $22 for it but wouldn't sell it for any price!

The happy housewife, seen on the side of the Hand-I-Sift flour sifter, at left, demonstrates how good helpers in the kitchen (a dutiful son and daughter) and the right kitchen tool in hand can turn out not only the perfect pie but the perfect life. Mixers, can openers, cutting boards, magnets, ice-cream scoops, burger molds, spatulas, timers, clocks, and toasters—kitchen "gadgets"—had started to infiltrate the housewife's life and fill the nooks and crannies of her kitchen by the 1950s. Though many are gone from the high-tech kitchens of today, Judy Kaminsky's Cookin', a cozy, cluttered warehouse of recycled gourmet appurtenances in San Francisco, Carol Levison's Once Upon a Table, in Pittsfield, Massachusetts, a supplier of vintage kitchenalia (and the flour sifter at left), and Riverside Housewares, a traditional kitchen retailer in New York City that trades up-to-date items for secondhand originals (like the Pyrex coffeepot on page 215) all are proof that what goes around comes around—especially in the kitchen.

Preceding pages: From Carol Levison's Once Upon a Table, at left, comes this KitchenAid mixer, which was bought new in the 1970s for about $200. "It was originally a dreary Harvest Gold until I took it to a sympathetic auto refinisher and had him make it into a yellow Corvette!" At right, her Vac-O-Mat portable can opener, manufactured by the Rival Manufacturing Co., Kansas City, Missouri. She paid $20 for it ten years ago.

Above: A quartet of electric toasters from the 1950s, gleaming in the California sun at the Long Beach Outdoor Market. Before purchasing a vintage appliance, check the cord and plug, and if possible, plug it in and see if the internal coils heat up. (See photographer in reflection!)

Right: Just what your old appliances may be in the market for: an electric cord. These cords from the 1920s through 1940s, for toasters, waffle irons, electric coffeepots, and corn poppers, have "wonderful Bakelite parts in red and black and fantastic geometric patterns on the cords themselves," boasts Carol Levison, their proud owner. They cost from $5 to $15 each.

Above: Stephen Drucker's phony package of Golden Crust sliced bread suits perfectly what he refers to as his *Life* magazine 1948-style kitchen (see page 58 to revisit). A picture of a Sunbeam toaster found in a skimmed 1951 issue of *Good Housekeeping* triggers memories of the one that popped out the toast in our childhood kitchen. My favorite was created not in our toaster but in the oven. It was sliced Wonder white bread dotted with generous pads of butter and sprinkled with a thick layer of cinnamon sugar.

Top left: Mark Campbell's Dualite chrome toaster is a new version of the great old English classic. You can find one just like it at Williams-Sonoma or other fine kitchen houseware suppliers.

Bottom left: Every respectable toaster in the 1950s needed to cover itself fashionably. Lisa Durfee's answer to that: a plastic toaster cover sporting a pair of très chic yellow French poodles. Similar kitchen kitsch (like the plastic farm curtains seen at the far right) can be found in her new outpost at the Germantown Antiques Barn, Germantown, New York. The larger of the two miniature toasters, the one boasting an electric cord, is a child's toy appliance, from Madalin, Tivoli, New York, for $8. The tiny toaster, $10 at the Long Beach Outdoor Market, Long Beach, California, dispenses salt and pepper out of the light and dark pieces of toast. The pouch of veggie potholders was seen earlier on page 165.

Right: Cutting boards must have been the number one Skil saw project in school shop classes. The crying onion wins my prize for the most original. I plucked it out of a lucky box at The Rummage Shoppe, Millerton, New York, for $2. Of course I slice my onions on it, and of course I cry, but now never alone!

Opposite, clockwise from top left: 1. A more legitimate cutting board, fairly commonplace in English flea markets, which is where Carol Levison of Once Upon a Table found this one. The carved wheat sheaf border adds to its uniqueness and the cost, $65. The wooden-handled knife unmistakably designated for bread was another English import for $35. The figurative set of sandwich markers, intended to identify an assorted platter of luncheon choices from chicken to egg, are from Carol's private collection, discovered in a dusty shop in southeast Massachusetts. She invested $18 and loves to have them around as a "1950s icon of the good hostess." (See a fuller view back on page 178.) **2.** Stacked on the kitchen counter of Mark Campbell's island retreat (see pages 48–59) is a hardy family of cutting boards. The most diminutive, detailed with a double fishhead handle, is a favorite for slicing lemons and limes. He found it for $3 at Kitschen, New York City. **3.** I found the cousin to Carol Levison's cutting board, seen in the top left corner, at the Bermondsey flea market, outside London, over a decade ago for about $10. The butcher-block piece under it was a leftover from the butcher-block counters that roam the periphery of our country kitchen. **4.** Without question it is the pineapple cutting board, the second of my New York trio, that I reach for most often. It was a fourth-grade project given to me by my son Sam.

When Carter and Sam, my two sons, were in the *Sesame Street* stage, they used the fridge front as a blackboard for their alphabet and numbers magnets. During the nursery school years they used them to mount their fingerpaint and crayon masterpieces. When Carter (and his mother) joined the Keith Haring fan club we totally camouflaged the front of the fridge with one of his subway art posters. Today fridge magnets have become toys for big kids. In the early 1980s Ataboy out of Los Angeles magnetized adult images, movie stills, and classic pin-up girls. Suddenly it was stylish to give and get magnets and transform the most dominant piece in the kitchen into something with style and substance. Now with grown-up alphabet magnets, like those seen at right and opposite, the fridge has gone interactive: You can send f-mail (fridge mail) to your friends and family.

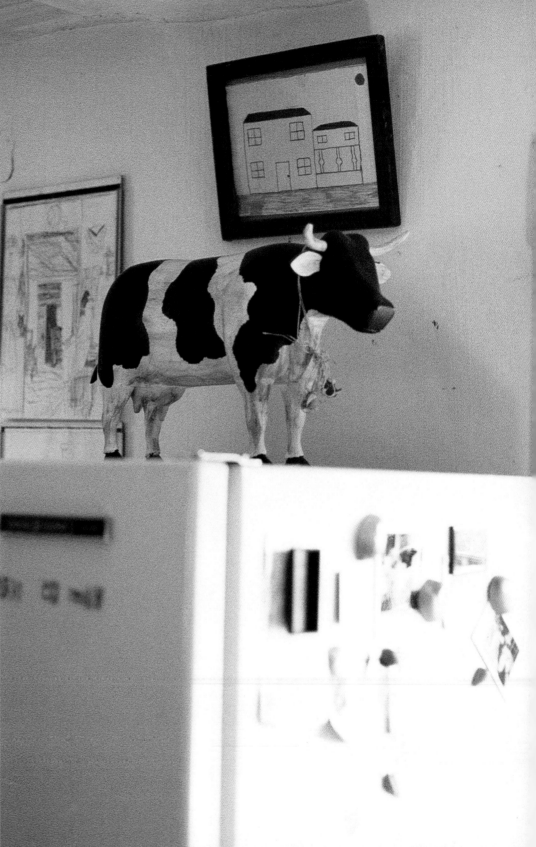

POLO · RALPH LAUREN

Be GREAT

THANKS FOR EVERYTHING

Unbeatable!

AWESOME

LOTTO

38223 298-05903058-10447

A 15 17 26 31 40 47 QP
B 01 16 27 40 47 52 QP
C 04 24 27 45 48 52 QP
D 09 11 17 34 36 39 QP
E 22 29 32 43 47 49 QP
F 07 14 17 20 37 54 QP
G 24 25 32 36 44 54 QP

we had a great
time with

Opposite: A pasture of Polaroids, a lotto ticket, thank-you note, and recipe card magnetically attached to the side of the old refrigerator in our country kitchen does not suit the grazing needs of the folk art cow (seen earlier on page 168) poised above.

This page: Close-up on the crop of magnets keeping things in their place on the side of our country kitchen bulletin board. The fruits and veggies were scooped up for 75 cents at the Community Thrift Store, San Francisco. The message magnets, adding a certain kind of "attractive" hieroglyphics to the inter-active thank-you note left by visiting friends, were a Christmas gift to the boys and are now committed to kitchen communications.

Junking is the journey. Meaning that it's not just what you discover but what you *might* discover and the trip that takes you there. The day I discovered the treasure trove of plastic kitchen gadgets at left I was on an uncharted junk journey. I was meandering down country roads on the Outer Banks of North Carolina and just happened upon Nannie & Pop Pop's Attic in the little coastal town of Shawboro. To discover a new resource in a junking territory I had roamed for over fifteen summers was in itself extraordinary, but to award it a junk level 6 was more than extraordinary: It was a junk miracle. (My instinctive rating system for junk emporiums extends from a top level of 1 down to 10.) Nannie & Pop Pop's was rated 6 by a complex set of standards that include external appearance and architecture, size, depth, diversity and uniquenesss of merchandise, creative clutter, and a big one: price! Price and size were pretty uncontestable in this shop, and when I came upon the plastic paradise in their kitchen section, the rating zoomed.

Left: Fridge frames, fruit magnets, an ice-cream scoop, a scraper spatula, a burger mold, two-way bottle caps, and a bag opener made the Nannie & Pop Pop "buy" cut because of their intact packaging. Baseball cards aren't the only collectibles whose value goes up when they're unopened. How about a never-been-opened, never-been-used burger mold? "Trade you for a Mark McGwire!"

If it doesn't work, you can always furnish a dollhouse with it. My thoughts exactly when I picked up this miniature plastic clock cupboard at a roadside tag sale for $2.

Above: A bottle of wine, an onion, carrots, grapes, cheese, and a clock? Yep, it's a battery-operated three-dimensional molded plastic 1960s pizzeria-style timepiece that I couldn't pass up for 75 cents at a garage sale in upstate New York.

After several years of never missing a second, our battery-operated kitchen clock died. A new battery didn't do the trick, so the challenging search for a replacement was instigated. I tried a few of my vintage electrics, but the cords were too short, and an extension cord made things overly messy. I vetoed a too-new-looking candidate Howard brought home. Finally, I found something that we all agreed on, but those clockless weeks had driven us crazy. Food was overcooked; schedules were flawed. I don't think any one of us appreciated how great a role a kitchen clock plays in timing not only our cooking but our lives!

Left: Designed to scare off gulls and keep pesky birds from nesting on docks or in barn rafters, these plastic predators watch the clock, waiting for dark. The object of their desire: a red-and-white-plastic Spartus, circa 1950, was a tag sale temptation for only $3.50. (Keep your eyes wide open, like my feathered friends, and you'll be rewarded with more than mice.)

195

Opposite, clockwise from top left:
1. South-of-the-border pottery plates were a box lot win for about 10 cents a plate at Copake Auction, Copake, New York. Not hot tamales but close seconds: green pepper and red tomato timers, $3 and $4, respectively, from Cookin', San Francisco. **2.** Clocks in the 1950s became billboards for products such as Hires root beer. I got thirsty at Bermuda Triangle, Nags Head, North Carolina, for $12. **3.** A classic electric wall clock spotted at an outdoor flea market may not be the bargain it seems for $5. Always check to see if the clock works, which doesn't necessarily mean it keeps time, and remember you'll be paying an electric bill; you can't pop in a battery. **4.** For minding those minutes on the stove (toy or real) and in the oven, a Lux minute minder. Though they still make them today, you can pick up a good-as-new one, like this one collected at the Elephant's Trunk Bazaar, New Milford, Connecticut, for $4. **5.** The kitchen timer blooming a daisy in the middle does time on a totally modern range top. Carol Levison of Once Upon a Table picked it up for $1 at a tag sale in Cape Cod. The fishmonger lady below is actually a spoon rest she bought new in Italy. **6.** There are days when you continually seem to run into the same category of item. My Sunday at the Long Beach Outdoor Market was clock day. It took me no time to make up my mind about this electric Westclox kitchen model with the original price tag, $6.98, and the style, "spice." **7.** If only I'd found this clock when our lives were filled with little blue smurfs! Instead of the kitchen (see it in one on page 23) I would have hung it in the kingdom of the smurfs, my boys' bedroom in the early 1980s. Origin: Penny Paid, Locust Hill, Virginia. Price: $4, and still ticking. **8.** A clock trio spread out smorgasbord style at the Long Beach Outdoor Market, are vintage 1950s.
Left: After World War II the kitchen became a much more glamorous environment. The popularity of pastels in the kitchen (see Mark Campbell's pastel table setting on pages 138–39) is reflected in this pair of down-and-out romantics, rescued from a box of junk at the annual Memorial Day tag sale at Copake Auction. True love for $5.

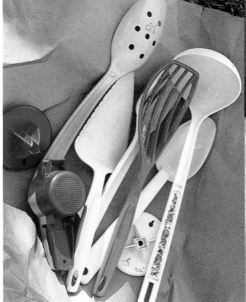

A CHEF'S CHRISTMAS TREE

My friend Gloria Landers began collecting old plastic kitchen utensils like those seen above when her son Perry, a chef in Kansas City, Missouri, announced he was finally going to have his own Christmas tree—a big one—in his loft there. Her vision for decorating the chef's Christmas tree was strings of little white lights and, for ornaments, large hanging kitchen utensils. She began collecting at thrift shops and garage sales. Condition and color didn't matter, but price did (she would need a lot of them), and each had to have a hole at the end for hanging purposes. She invested from 5 to 25 cents apiece. She sprayed them with two coats of paint in primary colors and hung them on the clothesline to dry. She then took very thin brushes and brightly colored enamel paints to transform them with white dots and stripes and whimsical borders into her own brand of kitschy kitchen folk art.

P.S. Gloria also suggests what fun they would be strung up at a bride's kitchen shower! Let each guest decorate one and sign it as a special favor for the bride.

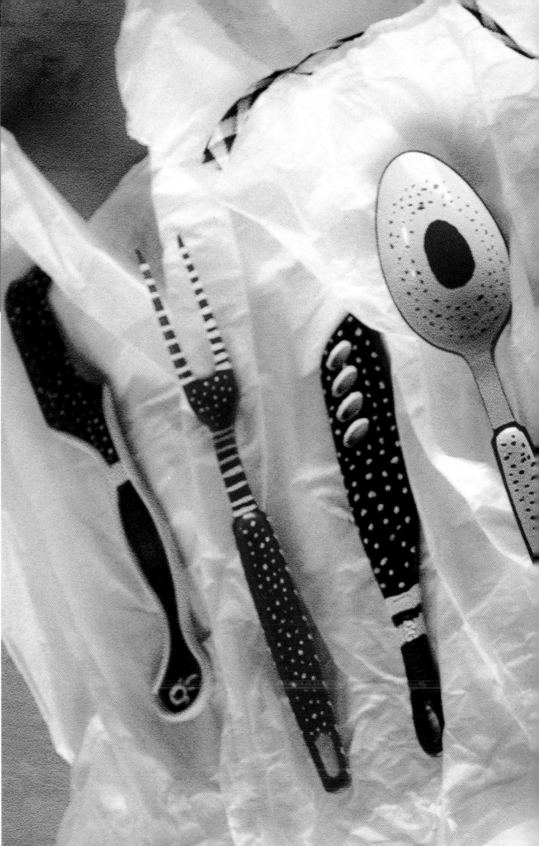

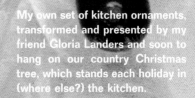

My own set of kitchen ornaments, transformed and presented by my friend Gloria Landers and soon to hang on our country Christmas tree, which stands each holiday in (where else?) the kitchen.

coffee break

For the two weeks out of the five summers Howard and I and the boys camped out in a large ocean-view loft in an old beach hotel on the Outer Banks of North Carolina, our kitchen consisted of a long eat-at counter with a stove, sink, and refrigerator tucked behind it. To us city dwellers, the kitchen seemed adequate, if not luxurious, considering you could see the ocean as you fried your eggs. We were at the mercy of the cookware provided, and I must admit the first morning I picked up the aluminum percolator coffeepot, I was more than a little concerned. I had never used a basic percolator, and failing at morning coffee could be a really disastrous beginning of the day, not to mention the entire holiday. After a good scrubbing (more tips on cleaning and using old coffeepots on page 207), I measured in the water and what I thought would be the appropriate amount of coffee, then placed it on the burner and prayed. When the water starting perking a light brown through the glass lid of the pot, my brother-in-law Hunter (he and my sister Nell were staying next door) walked in with a good morning followed by "Boy, that coffee sure smells good!" My coffee-making reputation was made that summer, and I owe it all to that old bent and tarnished metal percolator. I bought one in the hardware store before we went back to the city, but it never tasted the same there. It might have been the water, the salt air, or possibly the view that made it so unforgettable.

Above: From my mother's superb collection of junk masterpieces, a small (8" x 10") wonder exhibited in the guest house kitchen at Muskettoe Pointe Farm. She purchased it at Penny Paid, Locust Hill, Virginia, for an amount she wished not to disclose—75 cents.
Left: A sampling of my aluminum teapot and coffeepot collection. The little percolator at left was a gift from Charles Reber, an artisan of the Outer Banks. He used it for many years aboard his boat.

An all-aluminum lineup. From left to right: a coffee percolator, measuring cups and scoop, a teakettle, a measuring cup, a whistling teakettle, a coffeepot, molds, a percolator with a 1950s milk saver (when placed in the center of a pan of milk, it would whistle when the milk was hot) substituting for a missing top, and a four-cup percolator dwarfing a toy stove. Many were picked up at The Rummage Shoppe, Millerton, New York. Total worth of the collection: $25.

Sam Hamilton's real name is Margaret, but without a doubt she is Sam! I don't know if she was called Sam when the green mirror that now adorns her dining room wall at right was hanging in her childhood bedroom. She describes that room as having a kind of "pond" motif. The green mirror was embellished then with hand-painted lily pads. When she eventually moved it into her New York City apartment, the lily pads had to go. "I just kind of scratched them off." The pair of "curly" Biedermeier chairs, seen below the mirror, were from a set of six that she bought seven years ago from a friend of her sister's for $200, including a dining room table. The reflection through her looking glass is of her long, skinny kitchen (5$\frac{1}{2}$' x 12') and the top of her Ultramatic stove. Resting on top (see the opposite page) is a Michael Graves teapot that she begged her parents for when she was a senior in high school. Sam's love of kitchen things has not diminished. After recently exiting a big job in the world of fashion, she has now committed herself to the world of food. After an apprenticeship with a top chef in San Francisco, she plans to open her own restaurant and kitchenware store. The green mirror, curly chairs, and teapot will follow her there.

Opposite: The little bird that used to whistle on the tip of the spout of Sam Hamilton's teapot has long since flown the coop. It was not unlike the one seen on my teapot on page 207.

Above: Lisa Durfee's 1950s Hotpoint, snug in a cozy corner of her kitchen in upstate New York (see pages 146–49 for more), is a country cousin to my 1950s no-name stove in New York City. Both were inherited–hers with her house, mine with our apartment. The main difference is hers is electric, mine is gas. (More old stove tales on page 66.) And she got a bonus gift with hers–not the classic whistling teapot seen on the back burner but, even better, the glass-domed coffee percolator seen at the far right. The Moulineux coffee grinder was another freebie at a local yard sale. Better yet, it works. The little chalkware cat, not unlike my "bird of the range," seen on the opposite page, was 10 cents at a tag sale in Salisbury, Connecticut. The large heat-resistant aluminum pad covering to the right of the burners allows accessible stovetop storage. To keep the porcelain jacket of an old stove pure as the driven snow, Winsor Williams, the owner and savior of endless amounts of old stove souls at Antique Stove Heaven in Los Angeles (see page 68), recommends a glass cleaner or products such as Formula 409 or Fantastik.

Left: My mother is always worried about the trio of flea market masterpieces hanging over the stove in our kitchen in New York City. She's right. They probably are a fire hazard hanging that close to the gas burners. (Don't do as I do.) The large vase of chrysanthemums, an unframed oil on board, was bought six years ago at the Twenty-sixth Street Flea Market for $75. The little still life of peaches, to its right, is one of my favorite finds ever. The inscription, penned in longhand on the back, is as loved as the painting: "from Aunt Alice—who picked and painted them from a tree in her own yard in 1888." Below the peaches is my trusty folk art polka-dotted wooden bird, who is second chef to all our stovetop feasts. He was sent home with me after a coffee break in my dear friend Brigitte Lacombe's kitchen just around the corner. She felt he would nest more comfortably in the painted jungle of my kitchen than hers (which is quite spare and graciously peaceful). The nightingale perched on the teapot before him belts out a musical whistle as steam fills his lungs. It was a gift from friends and neighbors who live a little farther downtown, Riki and Bob Larimer, who also created and manufactured him. (For info on how to order, see Metrokane, under New York, in the Junk Guide.)

CLEAN COFFEEPOT COMBAT

Most teakettles today, like the one on this page, are made of stainless steel. If you can pick out your kettle or coffeepot in the lineup on pages 202–3, more than likely it's aluminum and requires a little more servicing. To combat mineral deposit build-up, don't let the water sit too long in the pot. At the first sign of a limey rim, attack it with a stainless steel pad and lots of hot water. Take a wad of paper towel to dry the insides thoroughly. The Vermont Country Store (see page 133 for details) offers a Tea Kettle Scale Collector for $3.95. You just drop the 2-inch cylinder made of finely knit stainless steel wire into the kettle to continually collect mineral deposits.

Most coffee makers suggest a heaping tablespoon of coffee per 8 fluid ounces of water. Coffee makers like San Francisco-based Hills Brothers and New York-based Chock Full o' Nuts used to provide a perfect little plastic measure right in the can to make the task fool-proof. The collection seen here was hand-picked at Cookin', San Francisco, for around 50 cents apiece.

HILLS BROS COFFEE

Clockwise from right: 1. According to one of my kitchen collectible price guides, the coffee grinder at right basking in the morning sun on my kitchen counter at Elm Glen Farm, is a Hobart's KitchenAid electric coffee grinder from the 1930s. Its version is priced at $30, but its version wasn't transformed into the unique piece of utilitarian KitchenArt (not just Aid) mine has. The base and screw top have been painted and decorated with the most charming floating coffee cups, and the spout has been perfectly finished with one perfect coffee bean. It was my one major find at the Pasadena City College Flea Market, Pasadena, California, one Sunday afternoon in 1996. Fifty dollars, at the time, seemed a lot, but the perfectly ground coffee it provides has been more than a payoff. Its not-shy grinding noise is the wake-up call of our household. **2.** When you met Sam Hamilton back on page 204, what was not revealed was the color of her hair. It's the same as her Wilma cup, a gift from a friend of her old roommate Tom, whose hair (not gender) was the same as Betty's. **3.** Stacked in the window of Sideshow in San Francisco are some novelty coffee cups for $5 each. I'm more intrigued by those displayed at the top of page 213, some for as little as a quarter. **4.** Meanwhile, back at Lisa Durfee's kitchen, a little ivy-colored cup rack picked up at an Adirondacks yard sale for 25 cents holds the mishmash of cups that were 10 cents each at a yard sale in Cooperstown, New York. The green apple sugar dish was a "couldn't resist" Pottery Barn acquisition for $16. **5.** The leaning tower of rainbow-colored Harlequin cups and saucers (not to be confused with Fiesta ware) were saved by Sam Hamilton from her grandparents' Cape Cod kitchen after it was sold. They live well on Sam's paint-spattered metal table, not far from Wilma and Betty, seen above.

1.

3.

5.

4.

Opposite, clockwise from top left:

1. No doubt about it, this cup's for Mom! No secret the price either, $10.50, since the price tag is still intact from from a recent junk journey to Kitty Hawk Thrift & Consignment, Kitty Hawk, North Carolina. Check it out in its eventual home on the table of my checkered kitchen in upstate New York, page 9. **2.** "You said you wanted half a cup of coffee!" is the message for these novelty half cups. "Mom's Half" I picked up at an estate sale in Falls Village, Connecticut, for 50 cents. "Pop's Half" I discovered sometime later in Kitschen, New York City. **3.** Orphaned coffee cups line the shelves of The Second Hand Shop in Geneva, New York. Note the very collectible diner cups on the bottom shelf. Check for chips and cracks before you adopt then run them through the dishwasher a couple of times before pouring in your first steamy cup of coffee. **4.** They're cheaper than paper. These secondhand plastic cups are from my favorite Rummage Shoppe, Millerton, New York. **5.** A hardy army green metal mug for coffee or a hearty sip of soup, $1 at The Rummage Shoppe. **6.** A welcome sight on those early mornings or late nights when you've plunked yourself down at a diner counter and before uttering a word the waitress is there with one of these and the pot of coffee in the other hand. They were $1 each at The Rummage Shoppe. (Or just about any thrift shop you walk into.) **7.** I could not pass up this testament to the power of coffee addiction and dogs. More than likely it will become a receptacle for loose change rather than the brew that gave it that coffee-colored stain. It was $10, at D's Place, Gloucester, Virginia. **8.** Wake-up rooster mugs, nearly new, for $1.50 each from American Junk, White Stone, Virginia. **9.** I prefer my tea or coffee out of a cup versus a mug. This one you won't find in the Wedgwood collection, but it's definitely in my Coffee Cup Hall of Fame.

My friend and fellow writer Abbie Zabar has a kitchen that floats in a large spacious environment that is open yet cozy, more timeless than contemporary, ordered but personal. If you had to pick the perfect Abbie coffeepot, it would be made of Pyrex glass. Eighty years after its creation by the Corning Glass Company, it is still functional and very contemporary in design. Abbie has in fact been collecting coffeepots, teapots, and double boilers for fifteen years. She loves, she says, "the way you can watch what's going on inside—kind of like the way my cats love to watch the clothes and soap bubbles swishing through the window of my washing machine." (Kind of like the coffee bubbling away in my Pyrex coffeepot at left.) Her collection started when Corning stopped manufacturing the pots. She bought every new one she could get her hands on and then searched for secondhanders. When she started hoarding fifteen years ago, she was picking them up for $4. Today, if she's lucky enough to find one in good condition, she could pay as much as $25.

A GOOD CUP OF COFFEE—FROM PYREX WITH LOVE

The Pyrex pot was Abbie's idea. She told me about Riverside Housewares and Hardware, New York City, a store that used to sell your everyday normal housewares. Then their clientele started to ask for Pyrex coffeepots and old-fashioned chrome toasters and a lot of the tried-and-true appliances you've seen in this book. According to Abbie, "a Handy Andy" sort of thing started happening in the back, which has now moved up to the front and even out front. Now the place specializes in housewares of the past to use now. On my first visit I pounced on the six-cup pot for $30, seen at left, then picked up a bag of coffee beans, ground them in my favorite 1930s coffee grinder (see page 210), used my favorite stainless steel 1/8-cup measure, seen at top, to fill the coffee basket with a generous scoop per cup, turned on the gas, and waited for that unmistakable "da-a-da-da-da" perking sound and the unbelievable aroma of freshly perked coffee. Thank you, Abbie.

into the woods

The woodpile kitchen snuggled into one of three stalls in our carriage house in upstate New York had been for the last ten years just a woodpile. Measuring 6' x 9', it could store little else except its original tenant, a horse. (If you are familiar with *American Junk*, 1994, then you may remember my first fantasy created in another of these stalls on pages 11-19.) Against the north wall between two stacks of cut logs I set up the kitchen altar, an old cast-iron woodstove, then prayed to that stable lad in far-off England.

According to *Meriam-Webster's Collegiate Dictionary*, tenth edition, the expression "in the woodpile" means "doing or responsible for covert mischief," which is in fact what this chapter and this woodpile kitchen are all about. Mischief . . . warm and cozy! When I read about Peter Wylly (*World of Interiors*, June 1989), a young college student who made a squatter's home for himself in an abandoned stable outside London, I, like his mother, cried, but for different reasons. I was so touched by his audacity and creativity in turning a ruin into a home of style and substance. It was Peter's stable and stacks of wood towering against ancient wooden huts and cabins in Scandinavia, the Austrian Tyrol, the Adirondacks, Maine, and Montana that were the architects for my woodpile kitchen.

Preceding pages and left: The little cast-iron woodstove, handicapped by a missing stovepipe, was salvaged out of a tag sale heap in upstate New York for $5. The cast-iron kettle, likewise handicapped by the lack of a handle, was part of a six-piece collection (the rust came later!) purchased at Tomorrow's Treasures, Pleasant Valley, New York, for $30. The oil painting above, deframed before the ink was dry on the check (for $15), was a heartbeating buy from a flea market mall near Fort Walton, Florida. The ash shovel leaning to the left of the stove is one of a trio picked up for $5 from a giant tag sale at Villa's Auction Gallery, Canaan, Connecticut. The collection of cast-iron frying pans was contributed by my friend Alice Reid.

In my woodpile kitchen there are three more woodstoves. The first, seen on the top of the green-and-brown-porcelain—topped kitchen table, to the far right, is a child's replica concocted into a lamp. My friend Alice Reid sold it to me for $10 and then gave me the table for free. The second stove, to its left, is an even smaller child's stove I found in the bottom of a box lot of miscellaneous odds and ends from a Copake Auction winning bid. The third, a mama-size version to the other two, rests on top of a little wire table I converted into a hanging shelf. Missing a few of its pieces, it cost me $5 at a local barn sale. Leaning behind it is a primitive wooden scrub bleached the color of driftwood—$6 at a flea market. Below it on the lower shelf is a wire teapot sculpture discovered at the Long Beach Outdoor Market, Long Beach, California, for $12. It echoes the collection of wire strainers and baskets lined up on the wall to its left. The domed cake saver screen, second from the left, was collected at Northeast Antiques, Millerton, New York, for $6. The green coffee mug, 75 cents from The Rummage Shoppe, Millerton, New York, rests on top of a portrait of a long-haired Native American from Bottle Shop Antiques, Salt Point, New York, $5. Another portrait of a Native American is seen on the little cast-iron frying pan hanging at the far right. The black metal box seen on the far left corner of the table, from Way Back When Antiques & Collectibles, Canaan, Connecticut, has a unique latch made of an old nail.

Right: Searching for props on an advertising shoot in Charleston, South Carolina, I was escorted by native Carolinian and fellow junker Bob Yearick to one of his favorite hunting grounds—Linda Page's Thieves Market, Mt. Pleasant, South Carolina. Though stoves weren't on my list I couldn't help but spot the great hulk of cast iron—an elegant blue parlor stove—sitting near an outside ledge. I never even inquired about the price, knowing there was no way I could get it home.

Opposite, clockwise from top right:
1. Donald Patterson Weeks's (a fictional guess at D.P.W.'s identity) sturdy wooden storage box for stove tools was picked up at the Elephant's Trunk Bazaar, New Milford, Connecticut, for $5. **2.** Rusty remnants of table cutlery dug up from the time of the War between the States touched some nerve in my Southern soul as I gazed at them tossed helter-skelter in a box at D's Place in Gloucester, Virginia. Whose table had they once rested on? I rescued these few for 50 cents apiece and sequestered them wrapped in tissue in an old wooden box in our barn in upstate New York. One day when we build a real house on the shores of the Rappahannock River (see *Garden Junk*, page 218, for a look at our temporary shelter), I'll take them home. **3.** Alas, the Handy Andy tool set metal box found in the hodgepodge of a yard sale table for $2 contained none of the children's tools it originally stored. But I loved the portrait of the little worker in overalls and hat toting a hammer and saw and substituted a couple of my kitchen tools and old school rulers instead. **4.** D.P.W.'s box was unfortunately bereft of any of the tools that he had once collected, so rather than leave the flea market with an empty suitcase I went on a hunt to fill it. One stop at the booth of the Four D's (located in West Warwick, Rhode Island) did the trick. Spoons, spatulas, colanders, bottle openers, egg timers, flame tamers, scoops, whisks, and mashers found a space and weighed me down for a total of $20.

1.

2.

3.

Handy Andy

TOOL SET

Skil-Craft Corp. Chicago

4.

Above: A gas cooker, a smaller cousin to the one seen at right, bides its time at a summer yard sale, waiting for an old sentimental scout to reactivate its camp-out duty.

Cooking out is not the same as a cookout. A cookout is what you do on Memorial Day weekend or the Fourth of July with a batch of burgers, hot dogs, and a grill. Cooking out is what you do when you are camping out. You can build a campfire, tote a portable grill or an old two-burner stove, like the one seen above and at right, and fry eggs or sauté chicken breasts. Depending on the diversity of your menus, you must consider packing up the appropriate cookware. If chili is the campers' delight, don't forget a covered pot to stew it in. Thrift shops are crammed with leftovers from campers' mess kits. Choose from lightweight tin pots and pans, cutlery, plates, and cups. Set your table with a mix of eclectic items from tin to graniteware, and don't forget the fun of icing up your drinks in authentic old thermoses and coolers, seen at right and on the following pages. While you're at it, keep your eye out for handy old electric lanterns. (Make sure they're built for today's batteries.) Now's the time to get out of the kitchen and camp it up!

Where's the beef, hot dogs, bacon, and eggs? The stage is set for a great meal in the great outdoors with the perfect portable Coleman camping stove and all the trimmings. The gray graniteware frying pan and coffeepot were part of a collection from Alice Reid's Antiques in the Barn, Livingston, New York, for a grand total of $30. The two square metal boxes supporting tin camp cookers are lunch boxes that stack into a miner's portable meal case, $20 from American Junk, White Stone, Virginia. The green thermos with an aluminum drinking cup top is also from American Junk, for $18. The little green lantern, way past its prime, plays R2D2 to its big green companion.

7.

2.

1.

Clockwise from bottom right: **1.** Every cookout needs a watchdog like Charley. **2.** Wooden-handled cutlery, sturdy stuff for the outdoors, $20 for four place settings, Bermuda Triangle, Nags Head, North Carolina. **3.** Bottle openers were the miniature billboards of soft-drink and beer companies starting at the turn of the century. They were the promotional tools that took you right to the source. Value is based more on the brand than the item itself. Most range from $1 to $10. **4.** Built for the 1950s "get up and go" spirit, the thermos, especially the one-gallon jug in some variety of plaid, was the choice of sporty picnicgoers. Two for the road: a Playmate with aluminum drinking cup, $10 from The Twila Zone, Nags Head, North Carolina, and the classic preppy Skotch jug with plastic drinking spout, $16 at American Junk, White Stone, Virginia. **5.** *Thermos* means "hot" in Greek. It was invented in 1893 by a Scottish chemist to transport temperature-sensitive medicines to the ailing. By the 1950s almost every American schoolchild, worker, and picnicgoer would set off for the day with one packed securely in his or her lunch box, pail, or basket. This classic was $5, from The Rummage Shoppe, Millerton, New York. **6.** A VulKano flashlight with an unusual volcano relief design on the side (the only reason I bought it since it no longer spews light) was $5, at Bermuda Triangle. **7.** Built to withstand the elements: a sturdy pair of aluminum salt and pepper shakers, $4, from Bermuda Triangle (see another view in #5). The speckled granite-ware plates, resembling old pie plates from the turn of the century, were $2 apiece from Bermuda Triangle. The toughing-it napkins are black-and-white-checked potholders. **8.** A Redbird camping lantern, a tag sale throw-in for $3.50, was totally irresistible, since the cardinal is the Virginia (my home state) bird. **9.** A metal popcorn popper (what campout would be complete without burned popcorn?) spiffed up with a little yellow paint awaits its turn next to a vintage hamburger patty press—both compliments of Penny Paid, Locust Hill, Virginia, for $5.

Mary Randolph Carter's
JUNK
guide

More than a hundred of my favorite thrifter's **haunts from junking journeys—east to west. Just hope I wasn't there before you!**

CALIFORNIA

American Rag
148 South La Brea Avenue
Los Angeles, CA 90036
(323) 935-3157
Monday—Saturday, 10:30 a.m.—9:00 p.m.
Sunday, 12:00—7:00 p.m.

& etc.
1110 Mission Street
South Pasadena, CA 91030
(626) 799-6581
Thursday, 10:00 a.m.—4:00 p.m.
Friday and Saturday, 1:00—6:00 p.m.
Or by appointment

Antique Stove Heaven
5415 South Western Avenue
Los Angeles, CA 90062
(213) 298-5581
Monday—Friday, 8:00 a.m.—6:00 p.m.
Saturday, 9:00 a.m.—3:00 p.m.

Aria
1522 Grant Avenue
San Francisco, CA 94133
(415) 433-0219
Open daily, 12:00—7:00 p.m.

Bountiful (Go just to be inspired!)
1335 Abbot Kinney Boulevard
Venice, CA 90291
(310) 450-3620
Monday—Saturday, 10:00 a.m.—5:00 p.m.
Sunday, 12:00—5:00 p.m.

Community Thrift Store
623 Valencia Street
San Francisco, CA 94110
(415) 861-4910
Open daily, 10:00 a.m.—6:30 p.m.

Cookin'
339 Divisadero
San Francisco, CA 94117
(415) 861-1854
Tuesday—Saturday, 12:00—6:30 p.m.
Sunday, 1:00—5:00 p.m.

David Yarborough
1005 Mission Street
South Pasadena, CA 91030
No phone
Open daily, 10:00 a.m.—5:00 p.m.

Indigo Seas
123 North Robertson Boulevard
Los Angeles, CA 90048
(310) 550-8758
Monday—Saturday, 10:00 a.m.—6:00 p.m.

Jimtown Store
6706 State Highway 128
Healdsburg, CA 95448
(707) 433-1212
Monday—Friday, 7:00 a.m.—5:00 p.m.
Saturday and Sunday, 7:30 a.m.—5:00 p.m.

Johnny's Appliances and Classic Ranges
17549 Sonoma Highway
P.O. Box 1407
Sonoma, CA 95476-1407
(707) 996-9730
Wednesday—Saturday, 10:00 a.m.—6:00 p.m.

714 Chenery Street
San Francisco, CA 94131
(415) 334-2187
Thursday—Saturday, 10:00 a.m.—6:00 p.m.

Krims Krams
3611 18th Street
San Francisco, CA 94110
(415) 626-1019
Monday—Friday, 1:00—6:00 p.m.
Saturday, 12:00—6:30 p.m.
Sunday, 12:00—6:00 p.m.

Liz's Antique Hardware
453 South La Brea Avenue
Los Angeles, CA 90036
(213) 939-4403
Open daily, 10:00 a.m.—6:00 p.m.

**Long Beach Outdoor Antiques
and Collectibles Market**
Veterans Memorial Stadium on Conant Street
between Lakewood and Clark Boulevards
Long Beach, CA 90808
(213) 655-5703
Third Sunday of every month, 6:30 a.m.—3:00 p.m.
Admission: $4.50

Muff's
135 South Glassell Street
Orange, CA 92866
Tuesday—Saturday, 11:00 a.m.—5:00 p.m.
Sunday, 1:30—4:00 p.m.

Pasadena City College Flea Market
1570 East Colorado Boulevard
Pasadena, CA 91106
(626) 585-7906
First Sunday of every month, 8:00 a.m.—3:00 p.m.
Admission: free

Petaluma Fairgrounds Flea Market
100 Gross Concourse
Petaluma, CA 94952
(707) 765-0268
Saturday—Sunday, 8:00 a.m.—4:00 p.m.
(Look inside for Stuart Hyde—great stuff!)

Rose Bowl Flea Market
1001 Rose Bowl Drive
Pasadena, CA 91103
(213) 587-5100/ (213) 588-4411
Second Sunday of every month, 9:00 a.m.—3:00 p.m.
Admission: $5.00

**Santa Monica Outdoor Antique
and Collectible Market**
South side of Santa Monica Airport on Airplane
Avenue off Bundy Avenue
Santa Monica, CA
(213) 933-2511
Fourth Sunday of every month, 6:00 a.m.—3:00 p.m.
Early admission: $5.00 before 8:00 a.m.

Scavenger's Paradise
5453 Satsuma Avenue
North Hollywood, CA 91604
(213) 877-7945
Monday—Saturday, 11:00 a.m.—5:00 p.m.

Urban Ore
1333 Sixth Street
Berkeley, CA 94710
(510) 235-0172
Monday—Sunday, 8:30 a.m.—5:00 p.m.

Used Stuff
143 South Western Avenue
Los Angeles, CA 90004
(213) 487-5226
Open daily, 12:00—6:00 p.m.

Yountville Diner (A good place to grab a great breakfast!)
6476 Washington Street
Yountville, CA 94599
(707) 944-2626
Tuesday—Sunday, 8:00 a.m.—3:00 p.m.
and 5:30—9:00 p.m.

COLORADO
AA Antiques & Restoration
17648 Highway 550 South
Montrose, CO 81401
(970) 240-8118
Open daily, 10:00 a.m.—5:00 p.m. in winter
and 9:00 a.m.—6:00 p.m. in summer

Alderfer's Antiques
309 East Main Street
Aspen, CO 81611
(970) 925-5051
November 15—April 15 and June 5—September 15,
Tuesday—Saturday, 12:00—6:00 p.m.
Or by appointment.

Pattie's Antiques
17086 Highway 550 South
Montrose, CO 81401
(970) 240-9624
Monday—Saturday, 10:00 a.m.—5:00 p.m.

$2.00 each

Triple D Sales/Tracys
66422 Solar Road
Montrose, CO 81401
(970) 924-1954
Open most days; call ahead for hours

CONNECTICUT
Doug's Used Furniture & Antiques
264 Kent Road
New Milford, CT 06776
(860) 355-2952
Wednesday—Sunday, 11:00 a.m.—5:00 p.m.

Elephant's Trunk Bazaar
490 Danbury Road (also Route 7)
New Milford, CT 06776
Sunday only, 6:30 a.m.—3:00 p.m.
Admission: $1.00

231

CONNECTICUT (CONT.)

Kathy's Cupboard
414 Main Street
Winsted, CT 06098
(860) 738-7663
Monday, Tuesday, Thursday, Friday,
10:00 a.m.–5:00 p.m.,
Saturday, 10:00 a.m.–3:00 p.m.
Sunday, 11:00 a.m.–3:00 p.m.

Retro
266 Kent Road
New Milford, CT 06776   (860) 355-1975
Wednesday–
Sunday, 11:00 a.m.–
5:00 p.m.

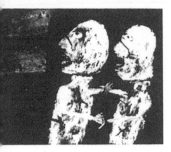

Shoestring
Antiques & Gallery

Ron & Susan Sloan

115 Greenwoods Rd. E
Rte 44 & Beacon Lane
Norfolk, CT 06058
(203) 542-1671

**Salisbury
Antique Center**
46 Library Street
Salisbury, CT
06068
(860) 435-0424
Open daily,
11:00 a.m.–
5:00 p.m.
Call ahead for
winter hours

**Salvation Army
Thrift Store**
129 Main Street
Danbury, CT
06810
(203) 792-9799
Monday–
Saturday,
9:00 a.m.–
6:00p.m.

Shoestring Antiques & Gallery
115 Greenwoods Road East
Route 44 and Beacon Lane
Norfolk, CT 06058
(860) 542-1671
Open daily

United House Wrecking, Inc.
535 Hope Street
Stamford, CT 06906
(203) 348-5371
Monday–Saturday, 9:30 a.m.–5:30 p.m.
Sunday, 12:00–5:00 p.m.

Villa's Auction Gallery
Route 7
Canaan, CT 06018
(860) 824-0848
Call ahead for auction times

Way Back When Antiques & Collectibles
Route 44 (across from the Canaan post office)
Canaan, CT 06018
Open daily except Wednesday,
10:30 a.m.–5:00 p.m.

FLORIDA

Country Village
11896 Wallsingham Road
Largo, FL 33770
(813) 397-2942
Tuesday–Saturday, 10:00 a.m.–4:30 p.m.
Sunday, 12:00 –4:00 p.m.

Douglas Garden Thrift Shop
5713 Northwest 27th Avenue
Miami, FL 33142
(305) 635-6753
Monday–Saturday, 9:00 a.m.–5:15 p.m.
Sunday, 10:00 a.m.–5:00 p.m.

Florida Victorian Architectural Salvage
112 West Georgia Avenue
DeLand, FL 32720
(904) 734-9300
Monday–Saturday, 9:00 a.m.–5:00 p.m.

Fran's Treasure Trove
167-A Eglin Parkway Northeast
Cinco Bayou
Fort Walton Beach, FL 32548
(850) 243-2227
Monday–Saturday, 10:00 a.m.–5:30 p.m.

The Hen Nest
5485 113th Street North
Seminole, FL 33772
(813) 398-1470
Monday–Friday and Sunday, 10:00 a.m.–5:00 p.m.
Saturday, 10:00 a.m.–3:00 p.m.

**Josie's Junk Alley
Thrift & Consignment Store**
MM 99.5
Key Largo, FL 33037
(305) 451-1995
Monday–Sunday, 10:00 a.m.–5:00 p.m.

Klutter Korner
538 Douglas Avenue
Dunedin, FL 34698
(813) 734-2429
Call ahead for hours

Little Ole' Lady Trading Post
314 Bayshore Drive
Niceville, FL 32578
(850) 678-7424
Monday–Saturday, 10:00 a.m.–5:00 p.m.

Pink Juntique
MM 98.2, Northbound, Oceanside
Key Largo, FL 33037
(305) 853-2620
Monday—Sunday, 10:00 a.m.—5:00 p.m.

Provence Art & Antiques
2620 Jewell Road
Belleair Bluffs
Largo, FL 33770
(813) 581-5754
October—April:
Monday—Saturday,
10:00 a.m.—5:00 p.m.
May—September:
Wednesday—Saturday,
10:00 a.m.—4:00 p.m.

Vanity Novelty Garden
919 Fourth Street
Miami Beach, FL 33139
(305) 534-6115
By appointment only

GEORGIA

My Favorite Place
5596 Peachtree Industrial Boulevard
Chamblee, GA 30341
(770) 452-8397
Open daily, 10:00 a.m.—5:30 p.m.

Scavenger Hunt
3438 Clairmont Road
Atlanta, GA 30319
(404) 634-4948
Open daily, 10:00 a.m.—8:00 p.m.

ILLINOIS

Betty's Resale Shop
3550 North Lincoln
Chicago, IL 60657
(773) 929-6143
Open daily, 9:00 a.m.—9:00 p.m.

Salvage One
1524 South Sangamon Street
Chicago, IL 60608
(312) 733-0098
Tuesday—Saturday, 10:00 a.m.—5:00 p.m.
Sunday, 11:00 a.m.—4:00 p.m.

KENTUCKY

Tickled Pink Memorabilia Mall
3269 Taylor Boulevard
Louisville, KY 40215
(502) 366-5577
Sunday—Thursday, 10:30 a.m.—5:30 p.m.

MARYLAND

Claiborne Ferry Furniture
10550 Miracle House Circle
Claiborne, MD 21624
(410) 745-5219
Call ahead for hours

MASSACHUSETTS

Blue Q
Pittsfield, MA
Manufacturers, not open for retail sales, but
check out Web site at: http://www.fridgedoor.com

Brimfield Market & Antiques Show
Route 20
Brimfield, MA 01010
(413) 245-7479
Open three times a year, in May, July,
and September, 6:00 a.m.—6:00 p.m.
Call for specific dates.
Admission: $3.00; $7.95 for guide (three issues)

The Buggy Whip Factory
Main Street
Southfield, MA 01259
(413) 229-3576
http://www.buggywhip.net
Open daily, 10:00 a.m.—5:00 p.m.
Closed Tuesday and Wednesday,
mid-January—April

The Hadassah Bargain Spot
1123 Commonwealth Avenue
Newton, MA 12154
(617) 254-8300
Mon.—Wed., 10:00 a.m.—5:00 p.m.
Thursday, 10:00 a.m.—7:00 p.m.
Friday, 10:00 a.m.—2:00 p.m.
Sunday, 12:00—4:00 p.m.

MASSACHUSETTS (CONT.)

The Little Store
29 State Road (Route 7 North)
Great Barrington, MA 01230
Closed in the winter
(No phone, no regular hours, but if you're nearby, check it out!)

Once Upon a Table
30 Crofut Street
Pittsfield, MA 01201
(413) 443-6622
Mail-order business, telephone calls welcome

MINNESOTA

uncommon finds!
Midtown Antiques Mall
Stillwater, MN 55082
(651) 430-0452
Monday–Thursday, 10:00 a.m.–5:00 p.m.
Friday–Saturday, 10:00 a.m.–8:00 p.m.
Sunday, 11:00 a.m.–6:00 p.m.

NEVADA

Art & Rubbish
250 West First Street
Reno, NV 89501
(702) 348-8858
Open daily except Thursday and Sunday,
11:00 a.m.–5:00 p.m.

NEW MEXICO

Gloria List Gallery
418 Cerrillos Road
Santa Fe, NM 87501
(505) 982-5622
Monday–Saturday,
10:30 a.m.–5:00 p.m.

NEW YORK

**Alice Reid's
Antiques in the Barn**
P.O. Box 113, Church Road
Livingston, NY 12541
(518) 851-9177
Call ahead for hours

Anne Keefe Chamberlin
County Road 58, Coleman's Station
Millerton, NY 12546
(518) 789-3732
Saturday and Sunday,
11:00 a.m.–5:00 p.m.

Anthropologie
375 West Broadway
New York, NY 10012
(212) 343-7070
Monday–Saturday,
11:00 a.m.–8:00 p.m.
Sunday, 11:00 a.m.–6:00 p.m.

Antiques & Collectibles
Route 44
Washington Hollow, NY 12578
Open daily, 9:00 a.m.–5:00 p.m.

Bottle Shop Antiques
Route 44
Washington Hollow, Salt Point, NY 12578
(914) 677-3638
Open daily except Tuesdays, 11:00 a.m.–5:00 p.m.

Bowery Kitchen Supplies, Inc.
75 Ninth Avenue, between 15th and 16th Streets
Chelsea Markets
New York, NY 10011
(212) 376-4982
Monday–Saturday, 10:00 a.m.–6:00 p.m.
Sunday, 11:00 a.m.–6:00 p.m.

Copake Auction Tag Sale
1/9/98

The Carriage Factory Antique Center
2348 Routes 5 and 20
Flint, NY 14561
(716) 526-4405
Monday–Saturday, 10:00 a.m.–6:00 p.m.
Sunday, 12:00–5:00 p.m.

Collector's Corner
Northeast Center, on Route 22, near Route 199
Millerton, NY 12546
Saturday and Sunday, 11:00 a.m.–5:00 p.m.

Copake Auction
Box H, Old Route 22
Copake, NY 12516
(518) 329-1142
Monday–Friday, 8:00 a.m.–4:30 p.m.
Call ahead for auction times

Exceptional Vintage
Kitchen and Table
Wares

English and French
Enameled Ware
Kitchenalia

Carol Levison
(413) 443-6622

ONCE UPON A TABLE

Pots
Pans

Fishs Eddy
889 Broadway (corner of 19th Street)
New York, NY 10003
(212) 420-9020

2176 Broadway (corner of 77th Street)
New York, NY 10024
(212) 873-8819
Monday—Saturday, 10:00 a.m.—9:00 p.m.
Sunday, 11:00 a.m.—8:00 p.m.

Fredie's Shack
4653 West Lake Road (Route 14 South)
Geneva, NY 14456
(315) 789-2931
Monday—Friday, evenings only, by appointment.
Saturday and Sunday, 11:00 a.m.—5:00 p.m.

The Garage Antiques & Collectibles
112 West 25th Street
New York, NY 10001
(212) 647-0707
Saturday and Sunday, sunrise to sunset

George Cole Auctioneers
53 North Broadway
Red Hook, NY 12571
(914) 876-5215
Call for auction schedule and appointment

Germantown Antiques Barn
(Has closed—call Lisa Durfee direct for an appointment
in her barn or visit her auction site on ebay.com!)
Lisa Durfee
Germantown, NY 12526
(518) 537-3437
on ebay.com—"durflink"

Hessney's Antiques & Used Furniture
405 Exchange Street
Geneva, NY 14456
(315) 789-0126; (315) 789-9349 for auction company
Monday—Saturday, 9:30 a.m.—5:00 p.m.

Howard Frisch
New and Antiquarian Books
Old Post Road, P.O. Box 75
Livingston, NY 12541
(518) 851-7493
email: hfhbooks@capital.net
Friday—Sunday, 11:00 a.m.—4:00 p.m.

Johnson's Antiques
Route 22 North
Millerton, NY 12546
(518) 789-3848
Friday—Sunday, 10:00 a.m.—5:00 p.m.

Kitchen Arts and Letters
1435 Lexington Avenue
(between 93rd and 94th Streets)
New York, NY 10128
(212) 876-5550
Monday, 1:00—6:00 p.m.,
Tuesday—Friday, 10:00 a.m—6:30 p.m.
Saturday, 11:00 a.m.—6:00 p.m.

Kitschen
380 Bleecker Street
New York, NY 10014
(212) 727-0430
Open daily except Tuesday, 2:00—8:00 p.m.

Madalin
55 Broadway
Tivoli, NY 12538
(914) 757-3634
Friday—Sunday, 12:00—8:00 p.m.
(or call for additional hours)

Metrokane
964 Third Avenue
New York, NY 10155
To order, call (800) 724-4321

Millbrook Antiques Mall
Franklin Avenue
Millbrook, NY 12545
(914) 677-9311
Monday—Saturday, 11:00 a.m.—5:00 p.m.
Sunday, 12:00—5:00 p.m.

Northeast Antiques
Route 22, near intersection with Route 44
Millerton, NY 12546
(518) 789-4014
Friday—Sunday, 11:00 a.m.—5:00 p.m.
and by appointment

Pottery Barn
(800) 922-9934
Call for nearest store locations or
to request a catalog

Riverside Housewares and Hardware
2315 Broadway (near 84th Street)
New York, NY 10024
(212) 873-7837
Monday—Friday, 9:00 a.m.—6:30 p.m.
Saturday, 9:00 a.m.—6:00 p.m.
Sunday, 12:00—5:00 p.m.

The Little Store

·Antiques·

29 State Rd (Rte 7)

ice's Barn $12

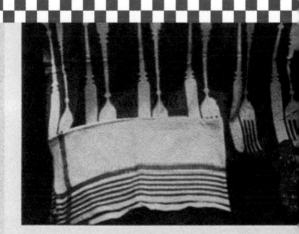
Dishtowels $2.00

235

Rodgers Book Barn
467 Rodman Road
Hillsdale, NY 12529
(518) 325-3610
Monday, Thursday, and Friday, 12:00–6:00 p.m.
Saturday and Sunday, 10:00 a.m.–6:00 p.m.

Ruby Beets Antiques
1703 Montauk Highway
Bridgehampton, NY 11937
(516) 537-2802
Friday–Monday, 11:00 a.m.–5:00 p.m.
and by appointment

The Rummage Shoppe
Route 22, North
Millerton, NY 12546
Open Sunday only, 11:00 a.m.–4:00 p.m.

Sage Street Antiques
Route 114 (Sage and Division streets)
Sag Harbor, NY 11963
(516) 725-4036
Saturday, 11:00 a.m.–5:00 p.m.
Sunday, 1:00–5:00 p.m.

Second Chance
45 Main Street
Southampton, NY 11968
(516) 283-2988
Monday–Saturday, 10:00 a.m.–5:00 p.m.
Sunday, 12:00–5:00 p.m.

The Second Hand Shop
19 East Castle Street
Geneva, NY 14456
(315) 789-7504
Monday–Saturday, 9:00 a.m.–5:00 p.m.

Skrookie's 5 & 20 Antiques and Collectibles
0857 Waterloo–Geneva Road
Waterloo, NY 13165
(315) 789-9245
Summer (July and August): Monday, Thursday,
Friday, Saturday, 11:00 a.m.–5:00 p.m.
Spring and fall: Friday and Saturday,
11:00 a.m.–5:00 p.m.

SoHo Antiques & Collectibles Flea Market
Broadway and Grand Street
New York, NY
(212) 682-2000
Saturday and Sunday, 9:00 a.m.–5:00 p.m.

Stan'z Used Items & Antiques
743 Ulster Avenue
Kingston, NY 12401
(914) 331-7579
Tuesday–Saturday, 11:00 a.m.–5:00 p.m.

Stormville Airport Antiques Show & Flea Market
Route 216 (between Route 55 and Route 52)
Stormville, NY
(914) 221-6561
Call for dates

Takashimaya
693 Fifth Avenue (between 54th and 55th streets)
New York, NY 10022
(212) 350-0100
Monday–Wednesday, 10:00 a.m.–6:00 p.m.
Thursday, 10:00 a.m.–8:00 p.m.
Friday and Saturday, 10:00 a.m.–6:00 p.m.

Thriftique
South Center Street
Millerton, NY 12546
(518) 789-6314
Open daily, 10:00 a.m.–3:00 p.m.

Tomorrow's Treasures
Route 44
Pleasant Valley, NY 12569
(914) 635-8600/8402
Thursday–Sunday,
9:00 a.m.–5:00 p.m.

22 Junk-A-Tique
Route 22
Millerton, NY 12546
(518) 789-4718
Call ahead for hours

Twenty-sixth Street Flea Market
Sixth Avenue and 26th Street
New York, NY 10001
(212) 243-5343
Saturday and Sunday,
sunrise to sunset
Admission: $1.00

The Watnot Shop
525 Warren Street
Hudson, NY 12534
(518) 828-1081
Monday–Saturday, 10:00 a.m.–4:00 p.m.

Williams-Sonoma
(800) 541-2233
http://www.williams-sonoma.com
Call for nearest store locations or
to request a catalog

Yard Sale
66 Newtown Lane (rear building)
East Hampton, NY 11937
(516) 324-7048
Saturday and Sunday, 11:00 a.m.–5:00 p.m.

HotLine Thrift Shop
Route 64
Manteo, NC 27954
(252) 473-3127
Monday—Friday, 10:00 a.m.—5:00 p.m.
Saturday, 9:00 a.m.—2:00 p.m.

HotLine Too
Milepost 9½ on the Route 158 bypass
Kill Devil Hills, NC 27948
(252) 441-1244
Monday—Friday, 10:00 a.m.—5:00 p.m.
Saturday, 9:00 a.m.—2:00 p.m.

Merry-Go-Round Thrift Shop
Milepost 9
903 South Virginia Dare Trail
Kill Devil Hills, NC 27948
(252) 441-3241
Monday—Saturday, 10:00 a.m.—5:00 p.m.

Nannie & Pop Pop's Attic
Highway 158
Shawboro, NC 27973
(252) 333-1220

Highway 168
Moyock, NC 27958
(252) 435-6011
Monday—Saturday, 9:00 a.m.—5:00 p.m.

A Penny Saved Thrift & Consignment Shop
3105 North Croatan Highway
Seagate North Shopping Center
Kill Devil Hills, NC 27948
(252) 441-8024
Monday—Saturday, 10:00 a.m.—5:00 p.m.

Teen Challenge Thrift Store
Dare Center Mall
1740 Croatan Highway
Kill Devil Hills, NC 27948
(252) 441-1412
Monday—Saturday, 10:00 a.m.—5:00 p.m.

The Twila Zone
3330 South Virginia Dare Trail
Nags Head, NC 27959
(252) 480-0399
Tuesday—Saturday, 10:30 a.m.—4:00 p.m.

Twisted Fish Ocean Art Gallery
1903 South Croatan Highway
Kill Devil Hills, NC 27948
(252) 441-5757
Summer: open daily, 9:00 a.m.—9:00 p.m.
Off-season: by chance or appointment

RHODE ISLAND

Countryside Consignments
332 7 Mile Road
Scituate, RI 02831
(401) 826-7926
Open daily except Wednesday,
7:00 a.m.—5:00 p.m.

The Gallery
1652 Main Street
West Warwick, RI 02893
(401) 823-1280
Tuesday—Saturday, 10:00 a.m.—5:00 p.m.

SOUTH CAROLINA

Linda Page's Thieves Market
146 Ben Sawyer Boulevard
Mt. Pleasant, SC 29464
(803) 884-9672
Monday—Saturday, 9:00 a.m.—6:00 p.m.

NORTH CAROLINA

Bermuda Triangle
Milepost 13½
Surfside Plaza
Nags Head, NC 27959
(252) 441-9449
Monday—Saturday, 11:00 a.m.—5:00 p.m.
Sunday, 1:00—5:00 p.m.

Charles Reber
Woodcarver
4600 South Roanoke Way
Nags Head, NC 27959
(252) 441-5307
By appointment only

TEXAS

Room Service
4354 Lovers Lane
Dallas, TX 75225
(214) 369-7666
Monday—Friday, 10:00 a.m.—5:30 p.m.
Saturday, 10:00 a.m.—5:00 p.m.

The Stardust
1133 East 11th Street
Houston, TX 77008
(713) 868-1600
Saturday, 11:00 a.m.—5:00 p.m.
Sunday, 12:00—5:00 p.m.

Tinhorn Trader
1608 South Congress Avenue
Austin, TX 78704
(512) 444-3644
Tuesday—Saturday, 10:30 a.m.—6:00 p.m.

Uncommon Objects
1512 South Congress Avenue
Austin, TX 78704
(512) 444-3644
Monday—Saturday, 10:30 a.m.—6:00 p.m.
Sunday, 12:00—5:00 p.m.

VERMONT

Carriage Trade Antiques Center
P.O. Box 1832
Manchester Center, VT 05255
(802) 362-1125
Open daily, 10:00 a.m.—5:00 p.m.
(closed Tuesdays and Wednesdays in the winter)

The Danby Antique Center
Main Street
Danby, VT 05739
(802) 293-5990
Open daily, 10:00 a.m.—5:00 p.m.

Vermont Country Store
Route 100
Weston, VT 05161
(802) 824-3184
Monday—Saturday, 9:00 a.m.—5:00 p.m.

Route 103
Rockingham, VT 05101
(802) 463-2224
Monday—Saturday, 9:00 a.m.—5:00 p.m.
Sunday, 10:00 a.m.—5:00 p.m.
To order or to request a catalog,
call (802) 362-8440

VIRGINIA

Alpha & Omega
Holland's Stage Coach Markets
and Antique Village
Route 17 at 1420
Gloucester, VA 23061
(804) 693-3951
Saturday and Sunday, 10:00 a.m.—4:00 p.m.

American Junk
This is the flagship store of
American Junk—y'all come!
489 Rappahannock Drive,
P.O. Box 1094
White Stone, VA 22578
(804) 435-1840, Call ahead for days and times

American Junk Journal
Good gab about great junk—a junker's newsletter
from yours truly! For information on it and other
junker's stuff (like an American Junk bumper
sticker) write c/o American Junk
P.O. Box 718
Millerton, NY 12546
or e-mail me at mrcjunkjournal@yahoo.com

Caravati's Inc.
Restoration materials from old buildings
104 East Second Street
Richmond, VA 23224
(804) 232-4175
Monday—Friday, 8:30 a.m.—5:00 p.m.
Saturday, 9:00 a.m.—4:00 p.m.

Jim & Pat Carter's Real Estate (If you decide to move
to Virginia with all your junk, call my father, mother, or sister Emily!)
Box 7, Chesapeake Drive
White Stone, VA 22578
(804) 435-3001

The Consignment Shop
Route 33
Locust Hill, VA 23092
(804) 758-2714
Wednesday—Saturday, 10:00 a.m.—4:00 p.m.

D's Place
Holland's Stage Coach Markets and Antique Village
Route 17 at 1420
Gloucester, VA 23061
(804) 693-3951
Saturday and Sunday, 10:00 a.m.—4:00 p.m.

**Holland's Stage Coach
Markets and Antique Village**
Route 17 at 1420
Gloucester, VA 23061
(804) 693-3951
Saturday and Sunday, 10:00 a.m.—4:00 p.m.
More than 45 shops

K & W Antiques & Collectibles
Box 2547
Jesse Dupont Highway
Kilmarnock, VA 22482
(804) 435-0542 or (804) 580-7827
Open daily, 8:30 a.m.—3:00 p.m.

238

RED CHAIRS $20

NOTES!

A most wacky place! They
leave everything outside year-
round. € I got my Define man-
nequin here—see photos? Naked
mannequins that reportedly
cause accidents, bathtubs,
sheet! everything. Summer
flea markets. Very unreliable
hours.
—50/50

MY WITS END

ANTIQUES

CARTONS / $1.00

King William Antiques and Refinishing
7880 Richmond Road
Toano, VA 23168
(757) 566-2270
Monday—Sunday, 10:00 a.m.—5:00 p.m.

L & C Owens Antiques
Highway 3
White Stone, VA 22578
(804) 435-6091
Monday—Saturday, 9:00 a.m.—5:00 p.m.

Lord Botetourt Antiques
6580 Main Street
Gloucester Court House, VA 23061
(804) 693-5402
Monday—Saturday, 10:00 a.m.—4:00 p.m.

Martha's Mixture
3445 West Cary Street
Richmond, VA 23221
(804) 358-5827
Monday—Saturday, 10:00 a.m.—5:00 p.m.

My Wit's End
12810 James Monroe Highway
Leesburg, VA 20176
(703) 777-1561
Open daily, 10:00 a.m.—5:00 p.m.

Penny Paid
Route 33, P.O. Box 26
Locust Hill, VA 23092
(804) 758-5280
Wednesday—Saturday, 10:30 a.m.—4:30 p.m.
Sunday, 12:00—4:30 p.m.

Richmond Antiques & Flea Market
449 East Belt Boulevard (at intersection of Belt Blvd. and Hull Street)
Richmond, VA 23224
(804) 231-6261
Indoor mall open daily, 10:00 a.m.—5:00 p.m.
Weekend flea market hours:
Friday and Saturday, 10:00 a.m.—7:00 p.m.
Sunday, 10:00 a.m.—6:00 p.m.

The River Market (A great place to eat!)
Rappahannock Drive
P.O. Box 1025
White Stone, VA 22578
(804) 435-1725
Monday—Saturday, 9:00 a.m.—9:00 p.m.

Secondhand Rose
1428 Hull Neck Road
Heathsville, VA 22473
(804) 580-2084
Tuesday—Saturday, 10:00 a.m.—4:00 p.m.

Williamsburg Pottery
Route 60, West
Lightfoot, VA 23090
(757) 564-3326
Sunday—Friday, 9:00 a.m.—6:30 p.m.
Saturday, 8:00 a.m.—7:00 p.m.

WASHINGTON, D.C.

The Brass Knob
2311 18th Street Northwest
Washington, D.C. 20009
(202) 332-3370
Monday—Saturday, 10:30 a.m.—6:00 p.m.
Sunday, 12:00—5:00 p.m.

Georgetown Flea Market
Wisconsin Avenue between S and T Streets
Washington, D.C. 20037
(202) 223-0289
Sundays, March—December,
9:00 a.m.—5:00 p.m.

WISCONSIN

Milwaukee Antiques Center
341 North Milwaukee Street
Milwaukee, WI 53202
(414) 276-0605
Monday—Saturday, 11:00 a.m.—5:00 p.m.
Sunday, 12:00—5:00 p.m.

Rummage-O-Rama
Wisconsin State Fairgrounds
Exit 306 off I-94, 86th Street exit
Milwaukee, WI 53204
(414) 521-2111
Call ahead for days and hours

Water Street Antiques
318 North Water Street
Milwaukee, WI 53202
(414) 278-7008
Monday—Saturday, 11:00 a.m.—5:00 p.m.
Sunday, 12:00—5:00 p.m.